Son of
Cheap Video

by

Don Lancaster

D1736227

Howard W. Sams & Co., Inc.
4300 WEST 62ND ST. INDIANAPOLIS, INDIANA 46268 USA

International Standard Book Number: 0-672-21723-6
Library of Congress Catalog Card Number: 80-51714

Printed in the United States of America.

Preface

Son of Cheap Video is the sequel volume to *The Cheap Video Cookbook.* Together, these two books show you very low cost ways of getting alphanumeric and graphics video out of a microcomputer and onto an ordinary television set.

In this book, you will find some major improvements, simplifications, and new ideas in cheap video. This new material will give you interesting and useful video projects and will deepen your understanding of low cost video display techniques.

In Chapter 1, we look at a video display system that you can build for your micro at a *total* cost as low as $7! This brand new, cheaper-than-cheap idea is called "scungy video." Among its other tricks, scungy video eliminates one or both of the custom PROMs used in cheap video, and it needs far less address space. Scungy video is also easier to interface to different micros and is much simpler and more versatile.

A super sneaky (and admittedly crude) way to pick up transparency shows up in Chapter 2. This is called "the snuffler" and lets you run video displays and compute at the same time without apparent interaction. *The snuffler can be built for under one dollar.* Its key part is a long piece of wire. With the snuffler, you can run a 16 × 64 or a 12 × 80 display transparently and still keep over 50% throughput for your regular computer programs.

Custom characters and graphics chunks are the subject of Chapter 3. Here we look at a do-it-yourself EPROM character generator, along with a plug-in module to let it fit your cheap video system. A music display that gives a detailed example of what you can do with custom graphics appears in Chapter 4. This music display system is useful for teaching beginning band and individual student instruments. It's also a good add-on to most any micro involved with music synthesis.

One of the most often asked questions about cheap video was, "How do I run on an 8080 or Z80?" A few answers appear in Chapters 5 and 6, where we show you how to run cheap video on these systems. We also show you schematics for an add-on circuit to put your TVT 6⅝ on a Heathkit H8 memory card. A companion keyboard serial adaptor, useful on many micros, is also shown.

Many of today's larger microcomputer systems lack lower case, and another natural question is how to provide a full alphabet display. Such dual case displays are essential for word processing and general business uses. We show you one answer in Chapters 7 and 8, when we plug a TVT Module A into an APPLE II to give you full case with simple mods and use of the existing keyboard. Total cost can be under $9.

As with the earlier book, we end up with an appendix containing details on the integrated circuits needed and some full-size PC patterns.

One important note before you go on. This is a you-build-it hardware book for hardware freaks. If you don't like hardware and don't want to involve yourself in video displays at the gut level, or aren't interested in super low cost above all else—then use one of the more expensive "mainstream" alternatives to cheap video, such as a crt controller system, a plug-in video card, or a ready-to-go terminal.

If you are not one of us, go away.

DON LANCASTER

Cheap video PC boards, kits, assembled units, and program tapes are available commercially from:

> PAIA Electronics
> 1020 West Wilshire Blvd.
> Box 14359
> Oklahoma City, OK 73114
> (405) 842-5480

A catalog and price list will be sent on request. Dealer inquiries are invited.

---

*This book is dedicated to the Encounter
of the Long Count Keeper.*

Contents

CHAPTER **1**

Scungy Video

The video display techniques we showed you in *The Cheap Video Cookbook* (Sams catalog number 21524) gave you all sorts of brand new ways to get words and graphics out of a microcomputer and onto an ordinary tv set. The cheap video ideas use a minimum of hardware and need a minimum of modifications to either the microcomputer or tv set. So, cheap video will be a very hard act to follow.

But, the earlier cheap video techniques were just a starting point. These ideas can be further simplified, made much more attractive and flexible, and made much easier to use. Since we'll need a name for these fourth-generation cheaper-than-cheap video developments, we'll call them *scungy video*.

What can scungy video do for us? For openers—

* You can now add a *complete* video display system to your KIM-1 or other "minimum" microcomputer for a total cost of $7 and using only five cheapie integrated circuits.
* You can free up practically all of the address space on your microcomputer, eliminating most of the address restrictions that cheap video seemed to put on your micro.
* There is far less interaction between computer and video circuitry. The video stuff now behaves as an add-on, rather than strongly interacting with your computer architecture.
* One or both of the custom PROM memories used in cheap video can be eliminated.
* The scungy video ideas are much easier to adapt to non-KIM and non-6502 systems.

* Nonmodifying scan coding can be used that is far simpler to debug and use and can be put permanently in PROM or EPROM.
* Full transparency with high throughput is now very easy to pick up.

As always, there are some tradeoffs involved. Scungy video may use the computer's interrupt structure, so managing *other* interrupts might get somewhat harder. And scungy video leans heavily on some other things inside your micro, particularly four parallel port lines and possibly an interval timer. But these are minor hassles and easy to live with.

The bottom line is this: *You can now put video on practically any microcomputer system at essentially negligible cost!*

Let's take a closer look at scungy video and see what it can do for us. First, we will look at the new secrets behind scungy video. Then, in Chapter 2, we'll look at a sneaky new trick in the way of transparency. Finally, we'll combine scungy video and the new transparency stunt into a transparent, super-simple, and very low cost video display system for you.

Much of what we will do with scungy video can be done by *removing* or ignoring parts already present on your TVT 6⅝, so very little will be needed in the way of new hardware.

HOW SCUNGY VIDEO WORKS

Scungy video is an improvement on cheap video. We still use the basic concept of putting a minimum amount of hardware between a largely unmodified computer and a tv set. We do this by letting the microcomputer itself provide almost all of the needed video timing signals. Our two key secrets of cheap video—the software *scan microinstruction* and the hardware *upstream tap* remain to give us an extremely simple video system architecture.

Scungy video *removes* parts from this in order to *add* two new secrets:

1. Scungy video may use interrupt or *break* mapping for the scan microinstruction, instead of the subroutine address space mapping used in cheap video.
2. Scungy video uses already available computer parallel I/O ports to simplify further the amount of special hardware needed. An interval timer may also be borrowed.

The typical cheap video architecture, as used on the TVT 6⅝, is shown in Fig. 1-1. Cheap video circuitry usually consists of seven or eight ICs on a small *interface hardware* card. The interface hard-

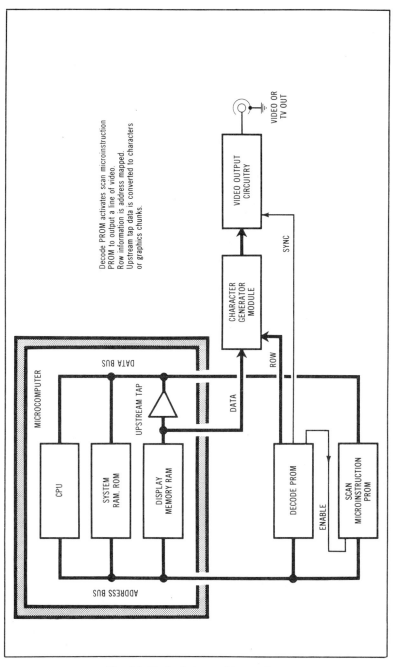

Decode PROM activates scan microinstruction PROM to output a line of video.
Row information is address mapped.
Upstream tap data is converted to characters or graphics chunks.

Fig. 1-1. Typical cheap video system.

9

ware card goes between the microcomputer and the tv set or video monitor. A small *Decode* PROM on the card decides when the computer wants to output a line of video dots. The Decode PROM in turn activates the *Scan Microinstruction* PROM, which takes over control of the computer long enough to output one line of video.

The Scan Microinstruction PROM causes the computer program counter to advance once per microsecond for the number of microseconds needed for a row of characters. During this time, the program counter is connected to the address bus, so *all* memory in the computer is also having *its* addresses advanced at the once-per-microsecond rate. This includes the display memory. Now, only the Scan Microinstruction PROM has access to the computer *data* bus, since this PROM is temporarily in command. But, the display memory is enabled as far as its *upstream tap*. This means that characters or chunks can go out the upstream tap while the scan microinstruction is taking place. As the characters or chunks go out the upstream tap, they are converted to alphanumeric or graphics symbols. For a more detailed explanation see *The Cheap Video Cookbook*.

Cheap video eliminates any need for a separate display memory or for complex stand-alone system timing. It does this by letting your microcomputer do all the work, time-shared with your existing programs. Cheap video also makes the display memory available to the computer at any time for any reason. This gives you a very fast interaction with on-screen information.

The two simplifications we need to pick up scungy video are shown as a block diagram in Fig. 1-2. Instead of the Instruction Decoder PROM, we use software and an existing parallel port on the computer. The parallel port directly outputs row and sync information for us, eliminating the need for a separate Decode PROM.

A small area in the computer address space is set aside as a *display* map. This display map is filled with scan microinstructions. These scan microinstructions are called by a suitable jump to the display map address space. As the computer is controlled by the scan microinstructions on the display map, the separate display memory is busy outputting characters or chunks through its upstream tap. Far less address space is needed by scungy video.

The display map *can* be a small PROM, identical or similar to the Scan PROM in cheap video. But, your display map can now be any old way to get the scan microinstruction code into your address space. You can use system RAM, ROM, PROM, EPROM, or direct hardware generation with a few LSTTL gates.

Scungy video's elimination of one or both PROMs dramatically simplifies our video circuitry, as we'll see in the upcoming examples. Besides making video displays even cheaper-than-cheap-video, scungy video is much easier to interface to non-KIM and non-6502

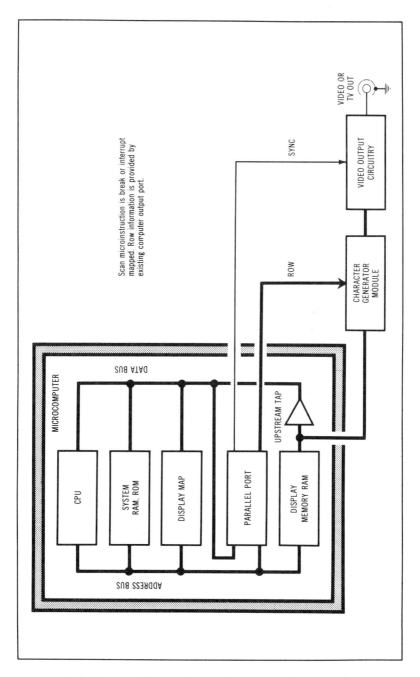

Fig. 1-2. Scungy video system eliminates one or both PROMs.

systems. It's also much easier to make fully transparent, as we will see shortly.

Break Mapping

Cheap video calls its scan microinstruction by a JSR or jump-to-subroutine command. While you *can* also do this in scungy video, let's look instead at a new approach and see what it can do for us. This other approach is called *break mapping*. Fig. 1-3 shows the differences between subroutine mapping and break mapping.

In Fig. 1-3A, we have the subroutine mapping we used on cheap video. On a 6502, the scan microinstruction is entered from the scan program by a subroutine jump. The microinstruction code consists of a bunch of LDY A0 or "load the Y register with the value A0" commands, ending up with a return-from-subroutine, or RTS, command.

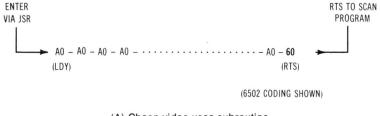

(A) Cheap video uses subroutine.

(B) Scungy video can use interrupt.

Fig. 1-3. The scan microinstruction can be a break-mapped interrupt in scungy video. Scan microinstruction sets number of characters or chunks per line.

The LDY A0 command causes the microcomputer program counter and address bus to advance sequentially one count per microsecond for the number of microseconds needed to put down a row of character dots or graphics chunks. Remember that while the scan microinstruction is advancing the address bus, the display memory is putting characters out the upstream tap and into the interface hardware.

On other microcomputer systems, comparable instructions are used to trick the microcomputer program counter into advancing sequentially once per microsecond as needed. Any command that doesn't mess up the status of the computer too badly will do if it is fast enough.

There is at least one other way to do a scan microinstruction. We can enter our display map by using a BRK or do-an-interrupt-now command. A BRK command in your computer calls for an immediate jump to the place that an interrupt would normally go to. In the KIM-1, the jump is to the address stored by the IRQ vector at 17FE and 17FF.

With break mapping, most of the scan microinstruction is the same as before, consisting of a bunch of LDY A0 commands. But, since we went into our scan microinstruction as an interrupt, we have to get back from it as an RTI command, as shown in Fig. 1-3B.

You can use either subroutine or interrupt to get onto your display map. Once on the display map, you output microinstruction code the same way. But, your exit from the display map has to match your entry. *Use RTS to return from subroutine and RTI to return from break.*

We'll look at scungy video examples using both break- and subroutine-mapped scan microinstructions. Which you use will depend on your particular preference in coding, and specific features you want on your own video system.

Fig. 1-4 shows more details on scungy video operation.

In cheap video, our subroutine-called scan microinstruction jumped to a different part of memory for every row of characters we wanted. Around 28K of memory was tied up and reserved for operation of the cheap video decoder. The location of this memory was also fixed in your system. The decoder would decide where in this 28K address block operation was to take place, and then it would output suitable row and sync commands to the character generator or graphics module.

With scungy video, we use either a subroutine or an interrupt jump to a *much smaller* space reserved for the display map. The display map is simply a single picture of the display format, expressed as one or more scan microinstructions. If you have only a single-line 1×32 display, your display map need only consist of 32 words. On a 12×80 or a 16×64 display, your display map can take around 1K of address space.

So, scungy video frees up bunches and bunches of computer address space for any use you want. The display map can go just about anywhere in your computer address space you want it to, eliminating many restrictions on what else in the computer goes where.

While graphics displays will take a somewhat larger display map (up to 8K for 256×256), the display map is still much smaller than the 28K tied up by cheap video. Taller alphanumerics, particularly

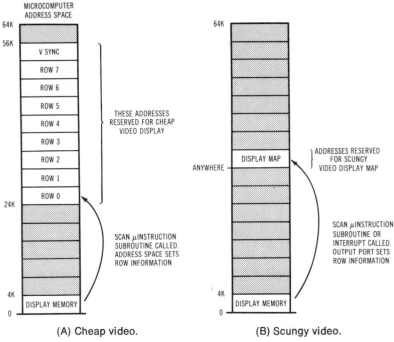

64K

56K

V SYNC

ROW 7

ROW 6

ROW 5

ROW 4

THESE ADDRESSES
RESERVED FOR CHEAP
VIDEO DISPLAY

ROW 3

ROW 2

ROW 1

ROW 0

24K

SCAN μINSTRUCTION
SUBROUTINE CALLED.
ADDRESS SPACE SETS
ROW INFORMATION

4K

DISPLAY MEMORY

0

64K

DISPLAY MAP

ANYWHERE

ADDRESSES RESERVED
FOR SCUNGY
VIDEO DISPLAY MAP

SCAN μINSTRUCTION
SUBROUTINE OR
INTERRUPT CALLED.
OUTPUT PORT SETS
ROW INFORMATION

4K

DISPLAY MEMORY

0

(A) Cheap video.   (B) Scungy video.

**Fig. 1-4. Scungy video scan microinstruction frees most of the computer
address space for normal use.**

12-line lower-case-with-descender characters, can now be done without any penalty in address space limits.

So, our first difference between cheap video and scungy video is often how we produce the scan microinstruction. We used a subroutine jump to a large 28K address space in cheap video, while we use a choice of interrupt or subroutine jumps to a much smaller *display map* in scungy video. Scungy video takes up much less address space, is far more flexible, and saves us at least one PROM.

The Display Map

The *display map* is an area set aside in your computer's address space to contain a replica of the screen display. When the computer gets on the display map, it will output scan microinstructions as needed to get the separate display memory to output characters or chunks in the right order.

A typical display map is shown in Fig. 1-5. Part of the computer address space is reserved for the display map. The display map is stuffed with scan microinstructions. The number of instructions received before the exiting RTI or RTS command sets the number of

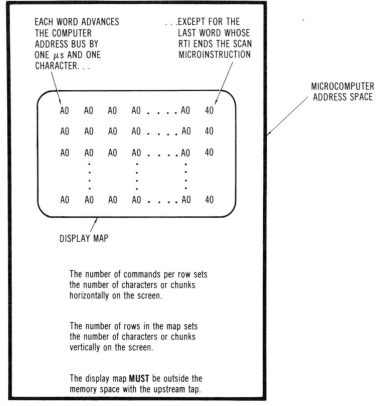

EACH WORD ADVANCES
THE COMPUTER
ADDRESS BUS BY
ONE μs AND ONE
CHARACTER. . .

. . .EXCEPT FOR THE
LAST WORD WHOSE
RTI ENDS THE SCAN
MICROINSTRUCTION

MICROCOMPUTER
ADDRESS SPACE

A0	A0	A0	A0 . . . . A0	40
A0	A0	A0	A0 . . . . A0	40
A0	A0	A0	A0 . . . . A0	40
A0	A0	A0	A0 . . . . A0	40

DISPLAY MAP

The number of commands per row sets
the number of characters or chunks
horizontally on the screen.

The number of rows in the map sets
the number of characters or chunks
vertically on the screen.

The display map **MUST** be outside the
memory space with the upstream tap.

Fig. 1-5. Scungy video needs a display map in the computer address space.

characters per line. The number of different scan microinstructions
decides the number of rows of characters or chunks on the screen.

To use your display map, you write a *scan program*. Every time
the scan program wants to output a line of video, the scan program
calls for a BRK or a JSR that jumps somewhere on the display map.
A scan microinstruction is then generated that outputs one line of
characters or graphics chunks.

*The lower bits of the starting address on the display map are the
same as the lower bits on the starting address of the display memory.* So, to output a different line of characters, you pick a different
scan-microinstruction starting place on your display map.

Now, while the computer is busy following the instructions on the
display map, the display memory is going ahead and outputting
characters or chunks by way of the upstream tap. Two things are
happening at once in your computer! These two things *must* remain
separate, since the instructions to advance the program counter are

15

obviously different from the video characters or chunks being output.

Because the computer has to do two different things at once, and if scungy video is to work, there is a most important rule about where the display map has to go:

The display map MUST be in a part of the microcomputer address space that is OUTSIDE the upstream tap on the display memory.

We need this rule to make sure that the scan microinstruction being fed the computer is different from the characters being output. In most systems, this is a trivial rule to follow. On the bare-bones KIM-1, this means that if your upstream tap is on pages 00 through 03, the display map must go outside this space. Two reasonable places to put it are in the RAM at 1780 or using a new small PROM on decoding K4.

All that is on your display map is a bunch of scan microinstructions. There are lots of possible ways to get your display map to appear in the computer address space. Four possibilities are shown in Fig. 1-6.

For instance (Fig. 1-6A), you can put your display map into existing system RAM. This is simplest, cheapest, and easiest. You just load the A0-A0-A0-A0 . . . . A0-40 scan microinstruction into system RAM somewhere. No new hardware or firmware is needed. The obvious disadvantage is that the display map disappears when the power does. But, this is a simple way to test a display and its format without any hardware involvement or commitment.

Or, in Fig. 1-6B, you can put your display map into existing system ROM, PROM, or EPROM space. A single large EPROM could hold your system monitor, display map, your scan programs, a keyboard encoding scanner, I/O routines, and so on. This option takes no new hardware, but it is best reserved till you are exactly sure what your system is to do.

Both of these approaches need one memory slot in the display map for each character or chunk on the display. But, since the display map consists of bunches of identical scan microinstructions, is there some easier way that we can use "mirrors" to make much more compact coding look like a whole display map? The "mirrors" are done by redundant decoding. In Fig. 1-6C, we use a small 32 × 8 PROM on a TVT 6⅝, either the existing subroutine-mapped PROM or a new interrupt-mapped one. The PROM is enabled anywhere on the display map as needed. The advantages of this route are that you are compatible with your existing TVT 6⅝, and only a single $1.50 PROM is needed for the entire memory map. A disadvantage is the need to custom program a bipolar PROM for each system you are going to use.

Finally, in Fig. 1-6D we use a plain old hardware decoder. This LSTTL circuit is activated when addresses are inside the display map range.

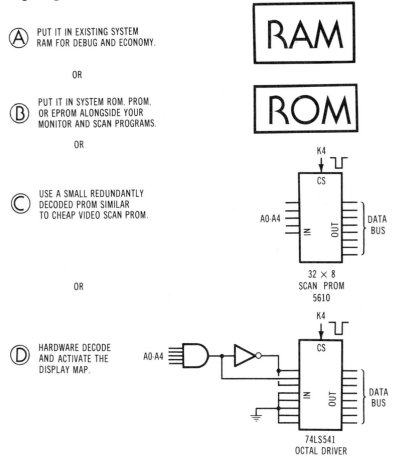

(A) PUT IT IN EXISTING SYSTEM RAM FOR DEBUG AND ECONOMY.

OR

(B) PUT IT IN SYSTEM ROM, PROM, OR EPROM ALONGSIDE YOUR MONITOR AND SCAN PROGRAMS.

OR

(C) USE A SMALL REDUNDANTLY DECODED PROM SIMILAR TO CHEAP VIDEO SCAN PROM.

OR

(D) HARDWARE DECODE AND ACTIVATE THE DISPLAY MAP.

Fig. 1-6. Four of many possible ways to build a display map.

If the address bus is outside the display map range, the data bus output of the hardware decoder is floated. If the address is on the display map but *not* the final microsecond on the line, an A0 is output. If the address is on the final microsecond of the line, a 40 (for RTI) or a 60 (for RTS) is output.

We'll look at examples of how to do a display map in system RAM and small PROM shortly.

INPUTS			OUTPUTS							
			Q8	Q7	Q6	Q5	Q4	Q3	Q2	Q1
WORD #	WHAT DOES THIS WORD DO?	HEX OP-CODE	DB7	DB6	DB5	DB4	DB3	DB2	DB1	DB0
0	LDY	A0	1	0	1	0	0	0	0	0
1	"	A0	1	0	1	0	0	0	0	0
2	"	A0	1	0	1	0	0	0	0	0
3	"	A0	1	0	1	0	0	0	0	0
4	"	A0	1	0	1	0	0	0	0	0
5	"	A0	1	0	1	0	0	0	0	0
6	"	A0	1	0	1	0	0	0	0	0
7	"	A0	1	0	1	0	0	0	0	0
8	"	A0	1	0	1	0	0	0	0	0
9	"	A0	1	0	1	0	0	0	0	0
10	"	A0	1	0	1	0	0	0	0	0
11	"	A0	1	0	1	0	0	0	0	0
12	"	A0	1	0	1	0	0	0	0	0
13	"	A0	1	0	1	0	0	0	0	0
14	"	A0	1	0	1	0	0	0	0	0
15	"	A0	1	0	1	0	0	0	0	0
16	"	A0	1	0	1	0	0	0	0	0
17	"	A0	1	0	1	0	0	0	0	0
18	"	A0	1	0	1	0	0	0	0	0
19	"	A0	1	0	1	0	0	0	0	0
20	"	A0	1	0	1	0	0	0	0	0
21	"	A0	1	0	1	0	0	0	0	0
22	"	A0	1	0	1	0	0	0	0	0
23	"	A0	1	0	1	0	0	0	0	0
24	"	A0	1	0	1	0	0	0	0	0
25	"	A0	1	0	1	0	0	0	0	0
26	"	A0	1	0	1	0	0	0	0	0
27	"	A0	1	0	1	0	0	0	0	0
28	"	A0	1	0	1	0	0	0	0	0
29	"	A0	1	0	1	0	0	0	0	0
30	"	A0	1	0	1	0	0	0	0	0
31	RTI	40	0	1	0	0	0	0	0	0

Left side labels:
- Words 0–15: NOT USED FOR 32 CHARACTER LINES
- Words 16–31: USED FOR ALL LINE LENGTHS

659-KS64
PROM NUMBER

☐ = "0"
■ = "1"
(POSITIVE LOGIC)

6502 coding
Use for Scungy Video alphanumeric scans of 32, 64, and other unpacked lengths and most graphics scans

Fig. 1-7. Truth table for optional scan PROM 659-KS64.

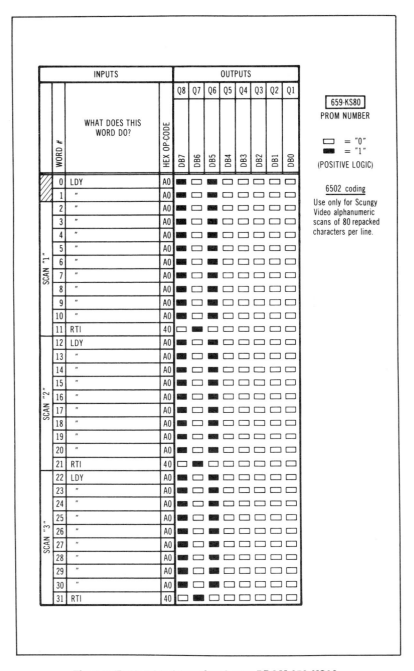

Fig. 1-8. Truth table for optional scan PROM 659-KS80.

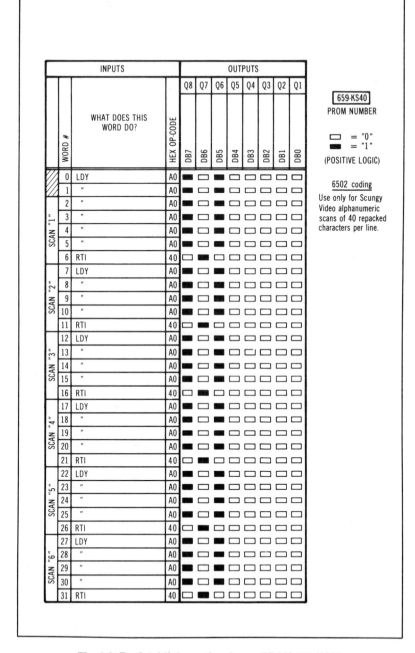

		INPUTS		OUTPUTS							
	WORD #	WHAT DOES THIS WORD DO?	HEX OP-CODE	Q8 DB7	Q7 DB6	Q6 DB5	Q5 DB4	Q4 DB3	Q3 DB2	Q2 DB1	Q1 DB0
SCAN "1"	0	LDY	A0	■	□	■	□	□	□	□	□
	1	"	A0	■	□	■	□	□	□	□	□
	2	"	A0	■	□	■	□	□	□	□	□
	3	"	A0	■	□	■	□	□	□	□	□
	4	"	A0	■	□	■	□	□	□	□	□
	5	"	A0	■	□	■	□	□	□	□	□
	6	RTI	40	□	■	□	□	□	□	□	□
SCAN "2"	7	LDY	A0	■	□	■	□	□	□	□	□
	8	"	A0	■	□	■	□	□	□	□	□
	9	"	A0	■	□	■	□	□	□	□	□
	10	"	A0	■	□	■	□	□	□	□	□
	11	RTI	40	□	■	□	□	□	□	□	□
SCAN "3"	12	LDY	A0	■	□	■	□	□	□	□	□
	13	"	A0	■	□	■	□	□	□	□	□
	14	"	A0	■	□	■	□	□	□	□	□
	15	"	A0	■	□	■	□	□	□	□	□
	16	RTI	40	□	■	□	□	□	□	□	□
SCAN "4"	17	LDY	A0	■	□	■	□	□	□	□	□
	18	"	A0	■	□	■	□	□	□	□	□
	19	"	A0	■	□	■	□	□	□	□	□
	20	"	A0	■	□	■	□	□	□	□	□
	21	RTI	40	□	■	□	□	□	□	□	□
SCAN "5"	22	LDY	A0	■	□	■	□	□	□	□	□
	23	"	A0	■	□	■	□	□	□	□	□
	24	"	A0	■	□	■	□	□	□	□	□
	25	"	A0	■	□	■	□	□	□	□	□
	26	RTI	40	□	■	□	□	□	□	□	□
SCAN "6"	27	LDY	A0	■	□	■	□	□	□	□	□
	28	"	A0	■	□	■	□	□	□	□	□
	29	"	A0	■	□	■	□	□	□	□	□
	30	"	A0	■	□	■	□	□	□	□	□
	31	RTI	40	□	■	□	□	□	□	□	□

659-KS40
PROM NUMBER

□ = "0"
■ = "1"
(POSITIVE LOGIC)

6502 coding
Use only for Scungy
Video alphanumeric
scans of 40 repacked
characters per line.

Fig. 1-9. Truth table for optional scan PROM 659-KS40.

If you go the small PROM route to keep compatibility with your existing TVT 6⅝, you can use the scan PROM codings of *The Cheap Video Cookbook* for your scan microinstructions if your scan microinstructions are subroutine mapped. If you choose to interrupt map your scan microinstructions, suitable new PROM codings are shown in Figs. 1-7 through 1-9. Again, these are *options*. Most likely, you will want to eliminate all special PROMS from your system.

The Output Port

Scungy video nicely eliminated cheap video's PROM instruction decoder. Unfortunately, we also eliminated any way to tell what dot row on a character we were working on, the sync signals, and the color graphics chunk select commands. Clearly, we need some new way to get these vital signals to the video interface hardware. Scungy video borrows part of an existing computer I/O port to do this. Two to four lines may be needed. Fig. 1-10 shows details of four options.

In Fig. 1-10A, we output port B0 as a composite V and H sync output. The alphanumeric row commands show up on B1, B2, and B3 in ascending order. Now, if you increment this port and then immediately decrement it, you will output only an H sync pulse. The pulse will be 6 microseconds wide instead of the usual 5 microseconds, but it still works well.

If, instead, you increment the port, delay for a while, and then decrement the port, so that the increment and decrement are around 180 microseconds apart, you output a V sync pulse. Both the V sync and H sync appear on the same port line as composite sync. Your positioning is done with software, and external hardware positioning is neither available nor needed.

Now, if you increment the port twice in a row, you still output an H sync pulse. But, at the same time, you advance the row counter by one count. You do this at the start of every live line to automatically step the row counter through the dot rows needed for a line of characters.

Here's a summary of the operating rules for your parallel port:

—To **clear** the port to no sync and the top (blank) character row, load all zeros.
—To **output only an H sync** pulse, increment and then immediately decrement the port.
—To **output only a V sync** pulse, increment, delay 174 microseconds or so, and then decrement the port.
—To **output an H sync pulse and advance the row counter**, increment the port and then immediately increment it a second time.

The port assignment in Fig. 1-10A is simple and works nicely for most graphics and short character lines. But it may be a bit slow for longer alphanumerics, or you may want to keep your H and V sync separate for hardware positioning. Fig. 1-10B shows another option. The row commands are immediately incremented with a single increment command, and a V sync pulse is output separately on a higher line. H sync is picked up in a separate blanking and TVT CS circuit that senses when a jump to the display map takes place. This option seems preferable for 64 and 80 character lines.

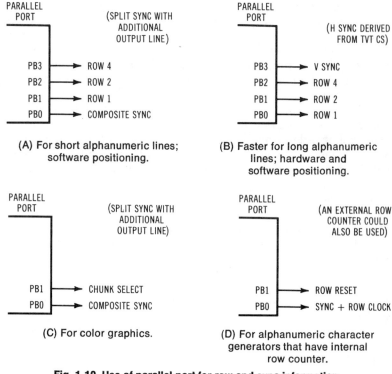

(A) For short alphanumeric lines; software positioning.

(B) Faster for long alphanumeric lines; hardware and software positioning.

(C) For color graphics.

(D) For alphanumeric character generators that have internal row counter.

Fig. 1-10. Use of parallel port for row and sync information.

If you are limited in your number of available ports, Figs. 1-10C and 1-10D show you how only two ports are needed for color graphics, or for alphanumeric character generators that have their own internal row counter. The *National* DM-8678 is one example. You can also add your own CMOS or LSTTL binary counter to save on port pins if you want to. In operation, one port is used to output composite sync and a row clock. The second port is used to reset the row counter when needed.

A BOTTOM LINE SCUNGY VIDEO SYSTEM

Let's see just how we can go about using scungy video. As an excercise in crudeness, let's pretend that we have only a KIM-1 and, say $7, and that we want to see what the absolute minimum is that we can do to get *any* video at all out of a microcomputer. We'll first set our sights rather low—a single nontransparent line of 32 characters.

Once we see what the bare minimum we need in the way of video really is, it is a simple matter to pick up all of the features of just about any fancier display we want.

Our bottom line KIM-1 scungy video circuit appears in Fig. 1-11, and a complete parts list is shown in Chart 1-1. As the parts list shows, very little is needed, and practically all that is needed is already available on your TVT 6⅝. A total of five integrated circuits is involved!

You can build up this circuit by taking your TVT 6⅝ and *removing* IC1, IC2, IC3, and IC5, and then tieing into the sockets as

Chart 1-1. Parts List for Bottom Line Scungy Video System

Integrated Circuits
2513 Character Generator
74165 TTL Shift Register
74LS04 TTL Hex Inverter
*74LS08 TTL AND Gate
*74LS02 TTL NOR Gate

Resistors
47
100
220
330
470 (2)
1K
4.7K

Capacitors
33 pF Poly
62 pF Poly
1200 pF Poly
0.001 μF (Optional)
0.1 μF Bypass
1.0 μF (Optional)
33 μF Tantalum

Diodes
1N4148 (2)

*Parts not already available on TVT 6⅝

shown by the bracketed numbers. If you start from scratch instead, your total cost, using surplus parts, should be around $7 or so.

The scungy video interface hardware has to receive characters from an upstream tap on your computer, and then convert these ASCII characters into parallel video with a 2513 character generator. The parallel video dots are then converted into serial video with a 74165 shift register and output to a tv set or video monitor. *Load* and *clock* commands are generated for the shift register by a 74LS04 that takes the computer's 1-MHz clock, and then derives a load pulse and seven clock pulses from each clock cycle.

Some additional gates are needed to get this bottom line system to work. A 74LS02 is used to activate the computer display memory (KIM pages 00 through 03) whenever the computer wants memory access, and whenever the video circuitry wants the characters to go out the upstream tap.

Our first programming example will have the display map sitting in RAM starting at 1780. A *NOR* decoding of AB6 and K5 will go high when the computer goes onto the display map. This new TVT chip-select signal gets combined with the existing K0 decoding to drive the display memory chip selects low *either* when the computer needs access *or* when the video circuitry wants characters to go out the upstream tap.

A final gate in the package is used to invert the composite sync that the scan software is going to output on port PA0. This inverted composite sync is then used in the resistor-diode video combiner circuit as shown.

These four integrated circuits are all we need to get video out of a KIM-1, but, if we do nothing further, a few extra characters will be displayed on the screen, outside the live message area. A little black tape is one cheap but crude way around this, but even on a bottom line system, something better is needed.

Why the extra characters? The extra characters come about since the parallel port row commands change to a nonblank line *before* the computer moves onto the display map and scan microinstruction. These row commands also remain nonblank *after* exiting the scan microinstruction. This is different from cheap video, where the row commands started and stopped exactly with the scan microinstruction.

So, scungy video needs a new blanking circuit, done with a 74LS08 AND gate as shown. The apparently "extra" line AB7 going to the blanking circuit takes care of a quirk of the KIM-1. The IRQ vector is stashed close enough to the display map that some extra decoding is needed to separate the two.

There are two capacitors shown in the video combiner. The 0.001 is a very crude bandwidth enhancer and is adjusted for the best

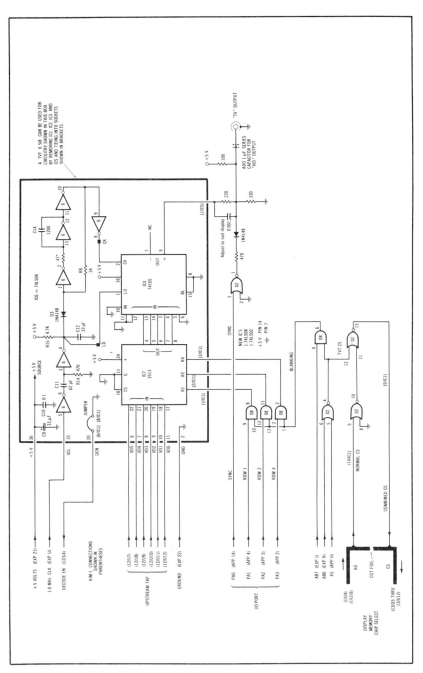

Fig. 1-11. Bottom line scungy video system.

looking characters on a tv display. Chances are that you will want to omit this capacitor entirely if a quality video monitor is used. The output coupling capacitor should be included for video monitor use and excluded for tv-set use. If you direct couple for tv use, the output voltage will be pretranslated to the bias level needed for the first video stage of a typical tv set. This output level is around +4 volts for white, +3.25 volts for black, and +3 volts for sync. See *The Cheap Video Cookbook* for more interface details.

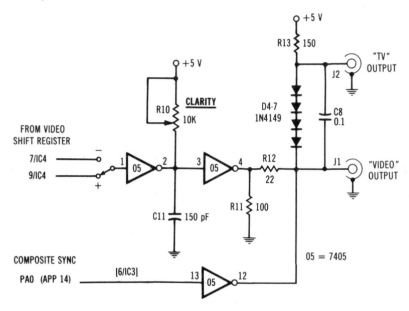

Fig. 1-12. A better video output circuit using parts from the TVT 6⅝.

Actually, we've done this particular output circuit just to see how cheap we can get and still have the circuit work. A much better output circuit is shown in Fig. 1-12. This better output circuit uses more of the parts already on your TVT 6⅝ and gives a full CLARITY control and an adjustable WIDTH control. You can get the adjustable width simply by using the TVT 6⅝ WIDTH pot instead of the 47-ohm resistor shown in Fig. 1-11.

If you want a winking cursor, return IC3 to its socket, but bend pin 6 up and out so that it doesn't interfere with the new sync lead.

Scan Software

Now, if you build this bottom line scungy video circuit and plug it into your KIM-1, nothing will happen. This shouldn't be surprising, because we haven't gotten anything going in the way of scan software yet. Your scungy video hardware will only work when you use suitable *scan software* to make it go. This is just the same as in cheap video, where it took both hardware and software working together to get us results.

For our first demonstration program, we'll temporarily ignore transparency and assume that you are going to alternate your computer and display modes. We will need only a single scan microinstruction for our display map. For starters, we'll put our display map in RAM, since this is simplest. Remember that our display map has to go outside the upstream tap, and that the upstream tap on a bare KIM will cover RAM pages 00 through 03. So, the only remaining RAM is the scratchpad starting at 1780. This is where the scan microinstruction will be stashed.

If our scan microinstruction goes from 1780 to 179F, the characters displayed will be on page 03 and range from 0380 to 039F. We can show this easily enough, since the lowest address bits on both the display map and display memory must be identical for scungy video to work:

Display Map   (1780) 0001 0111 **1000 0000**
Display Memory (0380) 0000 0011 **1000 0000**

Since our upstream tap is across 4 pages, or 1K of memory, 1K of address space, or ten bits, must "match" between display map and display memory.

Your Turn:

> Where are all of the 63 permissible locations in 65K address space for a display map if your display memory is to go from 0380 to 039F?

Generally, when you are designing a scungy video system from the ground up, you have lots of flexibility in where you put your display map and your display memory. The basic rules are as follows:

* The display map must go *outside* the upstream tap area.
* All the lower address bits must match between the display map and the display memory. The number of bits that have to match is set by the upstream tap. If the upstream tap is across 1K of RAM, then ten bits must match.

* There must be no conflict between display map, display memory, and other use of computer address space.

Since we have a choice of break or subroutine mapping for our scan microinstructions, let's look at the break-mapped route to see what it can do for us. Break mapping uses a BRK-forced interrupt to put us on the display map. When we go on the display map, we do the scan microinstruction. While the scan microinstruction is being done, characters from the display memory are output by way of the upstream tap and converted to video.

We will use parallel port A per Fig. 1-10A to get our composite sync and row commands. Later, you will most likely want to change this to port B to make room for an ASCII keyboard input.

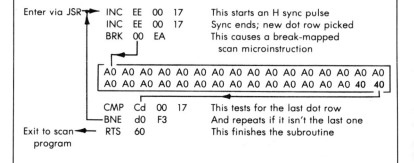

Fig. 1-13. Break-mapped subroutine for putting down an entire row of characters.

Before we look at the whole scan program, let's see how the critical part involving break-mapping can work. Fig. 1-13 shows a subroutine that will put down an entire row of characters. Each character row consists of seven dot rows of serial video. You call this subroutine as often as you need it, once for each row of characters on the screen.

To use this scan sequence, you have to set things up ahead of time. You do this first by initializing your port to be an output and forcing all port lines low. This means you are between sync pulses and the row commands are pointing to the blank top dot row of your character generator. This makes everything a blank before you begin.

Secondly, you load a value into the accumulator that matches the last line of dots you want to put down. For a 5×7 character generator, and the Fig. 1-10A port callouts, this value will be 0E. The zero part we don't care about, since these lines aren't in use. The E part of the number gives us between-sync and row seven with its 1110 code.

Finally, since you are break-mapping, you have to load your IRQ vector so that an interrupt will jump you to the display map. On the KIM-1, you do this by 17FE 80 and 17FF 17.

Once everything is set up, we can use our break-mapped sequence. As Fig. 1-13 shows, we immediately increment the port twice. This outputs an H sync pulse and moves us to the first live dot row on the character generator.

Then we do a BRK (00) command. The BRK command immediately calls for an interrupt, and the computer jumps to the scan microinstruction at 1780 and starts doing its LDY A0 routine. This makes the program counter advance one count per microsecond. Since the program counter is connected to the address bus and since the address bus is connected to all memory in the computer, and since the lower address bits match on the display map and the display memory, characters from the display memory will be output via the upstream tap.

As is usual during a scan microinstruction, the scan microinstruction has control of the computer data bus, but the display memory is simultaneously enabled as far as the upstream tap. This lets your computer do two things at once and is the key hardware secret to both cheap video and scungy video.

The scan microinstruction continues its A0s until we are two microseconds shy of where we want to end the line. Then we give a command to exit the scan microinstruction. This is an RTI (40) if you are break mapping or an RTS (60) if you are subroutine mapping. The last two characters on the line get output as part of the initial process of exiting either from interrupt or subroutine.

After we exit the scan microinstruction, we compare the port to see if we are on the bottom row of dots. If we are not yet to the bottom dot row, we repeat the whole process, putting down a new H sync pulse and then changing to the next dot row, and finally putting this row out as serial video. When the characters are finally complete, the sequence exits to the main scan program.

One detail. What is that EA following the BRK command? The 6502 rulebook says that a return from a BRK-forced interrupt goes **two** steps away from the point where you called it. Thus, the instruction word immediately following a BRK gets ignored. If this happens to be a two-byte or three-byte instruction, only the first byte will be ignored, and you find yourself in deep, deep trouble. A rule:

> **On a 6502, the slot immediately following a BRK command will be ignored. Always put an EA in this location.**

This break-mapped sequence lets us put down an entire row of characters in only fourteen words of code. The code is not self-modifying, meaning it can go in ROM or PROM. To change to a different row of characters, the IRQ pointer is moved to a different position on the display map. That causes a different match on the lower address bits, which in turn outputs a different part of the display memory.

A Timing Detail

How long does it take us to put down a single row of characters? Well, let's run the usual timing check. There's 32 microseconds of live scan time, 11 microseconds of BRK and RTI time (remember two of the RTI's 6 microseconds are charged against live character time), 6 microseconds for each of two increment times, 4 microseconds for the compare, and 3 for the branch. A total of 62 microseconds, just about what we would like.

But, hook this up and try it, and guess what? Your line is 67 microseconds long. This is still useful with a slight hold adjustment. But —where on earth did those extra five microseconds get burned up?

The answer is that the system monitor has to get its finger in the pie. BRK doesn't really branch to where the IRQ vector tells it to. It branches to the monitor firmware ROM. The firmware ROM then branches with a jump indirect to the address stashed in the IRQ location. This is typical of most monitors. The runaround is needed to keep the reset and IRQ vectors in firmware so that the system can be turned on and brought up.

The specific details of where the five microseconds goes in a KIM-1 are this. The BRK command, or any other IRQ, sends you to 1FFE and 1FFF in the monitor ROM. These locations immediately send you to 1C1F, also in ROM. 1C1F and the two following code words tell you to do a jump indirect to the location stashed in 1780, or 6C 80 17. Finally, the actual jump takes place, and the interrupt is ready to go. The monitor's piece of the action takes a jump indirect command and costs us five microseconds.

Another rule:

A break-mapped interrupt may take longer than you expect it to because of a monitor's operation. Allow 5 extra microseconds on the KIM-1.

To BRK and then to RTI will take a total of 18 microseconds. Two of these microseconds take place during the live scan, and 16 happen during the blanking and retrace time.

1 × 32 Scungy Display

A 1 × 32 scungy video alphanumeric scan program is shown in Fig. 1-14. This program works with the scungy video hardware of Fig. 1-11.

We have put this program on page 02, but it can go most anywhere you like, either inside or outside the upstream tap. There are only two limits to where your scan program can go:

* The scan program must not be on the display map.
* The scan program has to be separate from the actual memory slots displayed.

Thus, your scan program can even be on the display memory page. Unless you really want it to display itself, though, you'll have to have separate space for what is being displayed and the commands that cause the display to appear as video. Seems fair enough.

We start at 020E, do some equalization, set up the parallel port, and then do a V sync pulse. Then we do a bunch of H sync pulses, corresponding to the blank scans. We do not call any scan microinstructions to do this. We simply increment and then decrement the port to produce an H sync pulse and then use the delay loop starting at 0230 to space out between sync pulses.

When the blank lines are finished, we call our live scan sequence to put down the row of characters. The live scan is stashed at 0200–020d. Remember that the IRQ vector must point to the display map at 1780.

With scungy video, there is no longer any need to disable the Decode Enable or DEN line on your KIM. *Be sure to keep this line grounded.* One way to do this is to jumper 6/IC1 to 8/IC1 on the empty IC1 socket of the TVT 6⅝. Keeping DEN grounded eliminates many of the sources of bombed and astray programs you might have run across getting your older cheap video up. If you have a firm ground on DEN, you should be able to use a changeover switch without any program problems.

There *is* one new small quirk that comes up if you are using RAM for your display map. This RAM must, of course, be loaded with scan microinstructions every time you repower your system. But—

```
μP—6502              Start—JMP 020E     Displayed—0380–039F
System—KIM—1 +       Stop—RST           Program Space—0200–023F
        Scungy Video                              (64 words)
                                        Scan Space—1780–179F
                                                  (32 words)
                                        IRQ—1780 (17FE 80; 17FF 17)
```

Live Scan Subroutine:

```
        0200   EE 00 17    INC   1700     Output H sync pulse
        0203   EE 00 17    INC   1700     Advance row count
        0206   00          BRK   1780     ///DO SCAN MICROINSTRUCTION///
        0207   EA          NOP            Equalize 2 μs

        0208   Cd 00 17    CMP   1700     Is this the last dot row?
        020b   d0 F3       BNE   0200     No, do another row of dots
        020d   60          RTS            Return to main scan
```

Main Scan Program:

```
START→  020E   EA EA EA                   Equalize 6 μs
        0211   A9 FF       LDA   #FF      Make A port an output
        0213   8d 01 17    STA   1701        continued
        0216   A9 01       LDA   #01      Start V sync pulse

        0218   8d 00 17    STA   1700        continued
        021b   A9 0E       LDA   #10      Load last row compare
        021d   A0 1F       LDY   #1F      Delay for rest of V Sync
        021F   88          DEY              continued

        0220   d0 Fd       BNE   021F        continued
        0222   CE 00 17    DEC   1700     End V sync pulse
        0225   A2 EF       LDX   #EE      Set # of blank scans
        0227   48          PHA            Equalize 9 μs

        0228   68          PLA              continued
        0229   EA          NOP              continued
        022A   EE 00 17    INC   1700     Output H sync pulse
        022d   CE 00 17    DEC   1700        continued

        0230   A0 08       LDY   #08      Delay to complete blank scan
        0232   88          DEY              continued
        0233   d0 Fd       BNE   0232        continued
        0235   CA          DEX            One less blank scan

        0236   d0 EF       BNE   0227     Done with blank scans?
        0238   EA          NOP            Equalize 6 μs
        0239   EA          NOP              continued

        023A   20 00 02    JSR   0200     ///DO LIVE SCAN SUBROUTINE///
        023d   4C 0E 02    JMP   020E     Start new field
```

Fig. 1-14. Scungy video demonstration software—

Scan Microinstruction:

```
1780   A0 A0 A0 A0 A0 A0 A0 A0
1788   A0 A0 A0 A0 A0 A0 A0 A0
1790   A0 A0 A0 A0 A0 A0 A0 A0        (Fifteen LDY A0's followed
1798   A0 A0 A0 A0 A0 A0 40 40        by one RTI)
```

Notes:

Scungy video circuit of Fig. 1-11 must be connected to KIM-1.
IRQ vector must be loaded as 17FE 80 and 17FF 17.

Flowchart:

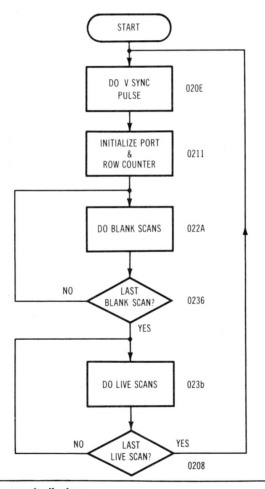

1 × 32 alphanumeric display.

since your display map does in fact map itself onto the display memory, **any writing on the display map will also appear in the display memory.** So, always load your display map **first.** After your display map is loaded, then go ahead and put your characters into display memory. Another rule:

> **If your display map ever has to be rewritten, the display memory will also have to be reloaded afterward.**

This creepy crawler only shows up if your display map is RAM. There is no problem with a firmware display map, so long as you or the computer never try to write into this space.

Your Turn:

Do a 3 × 32 scungy video display.

For more lines of characters, you have to make a bigger display map and have to change the IRQ vector for each line you want to display.

We will look at a 16 × 64 display after we pick up our new transparency trick in the next chapter. Any size or shape display you did with cheap video can also be done with scungy video, so don't let our short and simple examples deter you from using scungy video on sophisticated displays.

Your Turn:

Rewrite the 1 × 32 scan program to be subroutine mapped, rather than interrupt mapped.

Your choice of subroutine or break mapping depends on your programming style and the limits you have set on your particular computer system. Break mapping seems to be easier for generating short programs in nonmodifying code. But it also ties up the interrupt lines, is slower, and can be a hassle on graphics and other scans where lots of different memory blocks have to be called. Which way you go is up to you. Interrupt mapping is interesting, but right now, I like the subroutine route better.

Actually, *any* way you can dream up to get onto a display map and off again has potential for simple video displays. An addressing mode of JSR indexed indirect sure would be simple and handy. While it's not immediately available on the 6502, we'll find a way of faking it in the next chapter.

How about plain old jumps or relative branches? What about jump indirect? Can you use these?

What options are available to you? Is there really life beyond KIM?

CHAPTER 2

The Snuffler —
Super Simple Transparency

Now that we have slashed the cost of adding video to any microprocessor to under $7 and have freed up almost all of the micro's address space for any old use, and have gotten rid of some custom PROMs, what can we do for an encore?

It sure would be nice if we could have full and easy transparency with high throughput. This lets you compute and display at the same time. Full transparency without any critical program restrictions or lots of extra parts would be very handy.

It turns out there is a new and mind-blowing way to get full transparency on either cheap video or scungy video. All it takes is a long length of wire and a single extra CMOS gate! What you do is add a sensor coil to the *outside* of your tv set or monitor. The sensor coil tells the computer what the tv set wants to hear.

This new route to transparent cheap video is called the *snuffler* method.

One advantage of this snuffler method is that your cheap or scungy video interrupts your main computer programs, instead of vice versa. This is just like the front-panel interrupt common to some microcomputer systems. By changing the amount of time you service the display, you adjust the time left over for computer use. Your typical throughput time remaining can go as high as 95%, and often over half the time will remain for your other programs, even with a fancy display format.

There are some limits to the snuffler method, but these are easy to get around. To get the snuffler working the first time, some simple testing on your tv set will be needed, and you'll probably want to use an oscilloscope. You'll have to solidly understand how the snuffler works before you can use it. You will also have to do some interrupt management games on your system. And, you'll have to find some way to rapidly synchronize your microcomputer to an outside-world signal with a minimum of jitter.

On the 6502, you can get this rapid sync free with an obscure and often ignored input pin. On other computer systems, it may take some rethinking to get the same results. Let's try out the snuffler and see what it can do for us.

THE METHOD

If you have played with cheap video at all, you have almost certainly found out how unhappy the tv set gets with missing sync pulses, fast starts and stops of displays, misplaced timing, and so on. It looks like we have to always and exactly provide continuous sync signals to the tv set.

Or do we?

Let's take a closer look. Just *when* do we have to exactly provide continuous sync signals? Certainly during the live portion of a scan. No argument there.

We also want to continuously provide vertical sync signals at a 60-hertz rate without too much jitter. But this is a field or a frame rate and shouldn't be too much of a hassle.

Suppose we just *stop* delivering horizontal sync pulses during the blank portions of the scan. This is easy enough and lets the computer go back to working on its main program. And, the blank portion of the display will look—blank. The internal horizontal oscillator in the tv takes over, and the tv generates its *own* free-running horizontal sync pulses. So, there's no problem so long as the display stays blank.

The trouble starts when you fire up your external horizontal sync pulses from the computer at the beginning of a live scan. The result is usually a terrible looking *lock transient* that tears up the display, often in a wavy "S" shape or worse. If the lock transient is the same from field to field, you usually will get an ugly but stable display. If the lock point varies from field to field, you get a jumbled mess of lock transients superimposed on top of each other. But, you already know this if you've done anything at all with cheap video.

Now, suppose we eliminate the lock transient by picking just the right instant *with respect to the tv horizontal timing* to start a live scan. In other words, *suppose we lock the computer to the tv set instead of the other way around.* Now, if we do this and pick the wrong lock point, we will still get an ugly S-shaped display. But, by picking just the right lock point, we can get a nice, clean, stable display. We still have a lock transient, but we've made its amplitude *zero* so that it won't hurt anything.

In the real world, if we try this, the first few lines may still be bent a little or have some jitter. But, we can blank these bent lines and then start our actual display with the straight ones that follow.

Fig. 2-1 shows how the snuffler works. We add a pickup coil to the outside of the tv set to find out what the horizontal sweep is up to. The pickup coil will sense the horizontal flyback pulse. The best place for this coil is often the rear bottom of the tv's left side. After the flyback pulse is sensed, a CMOS Schmitt inverter or gate converts the pulse into something a computer can live with.

HERE'S HOW IT WORKS:

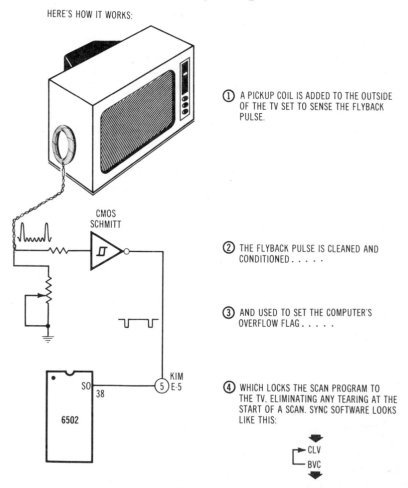

① A PICKUP COIL IS ADDED TO THE OUTSIDE OF THE TV SET TO SENSE THE FLYBACK PULSE.

② THE FLYBACK PULSE IS CLEANED AND CONDITIONED . . . . .

③ AND USED TO SET THE COMPUTER'S OVERFLOW FLAG . . . . .

④ WHICH LOCKS THE SCAN PROGRAM TO THE TV, ELIMINATING ANY TEARING AT THE START OF A SCAN. SYNC SOFTWARE LOOKS LIKE THIS:

CLV
BVC

Fig. 2-1. Snuffler feedback from tv to computer simplifies transparency.

Every time your scan software starts a new field, you hold up the start of the live scan on your computer until the next flyback pulse. This locks the start of your display timing to the tv's horizontal scan timing. You then put down a few blank lines to eliminate anything that remains in the way of jitter, and then go on to a stable live display of your choice.

There are lots of ways you can use this new "the tv set is ready" command. Shoving it into a parallel port or using it as an interrupt may be the only routes you have on some computer systems. Either of these two ways probably will work, but they might introduce too much jitter. For instance, an interrupt usually delays till the next instruction is finished, resulting in a 1- to 10-microsecond random delay. And, it's hard to read a port faster than once every seven to nine microseconds. While either of these obvious methods will work, the leftover jitter still may need bunches of blank lines before your live scan.

If your micro has a halt or a DMA command, maybe you can use this for fast, jitter-free locking.

The 6502 has a unique feature buried on normally unused pin 38. Haven't thought much about good old pin 38 have you? There it is, just sitting there halfway between 37 and 39, and unused in just about every 6502-based system.

Pin 38 of the 6502 sets the overflow flag *immediately* when fed a positive-to-ground TTL or CMOS transition. You can test for an overflow set in a single instruction, giving you a maximum lock jitter of around 2 microseconds. This is something the snuffler can easily live with and gives you a simple way to lock your micro to your tv set. Very nicely, the KIM-1 people even brought the SO pin 38 out to Expansion Connector No. 5, so you can gain access to your snuffler without any mods.

To use the snuffler, you interrupt your main program at the beginning of a field. Then you clear the overflow flag with a CLV command. Then you tell the computer to do a BVC 00 branch. This puts you in a one-instruction loop that continues until the flyback signal gets there from the snuffler. When overflow finally sets, you are locked to the tv set's timing, and are all set to put down a stable display.

The snuffler method works if

* Your tv set has reasonably stable horizontal circuits with decent lock recovery.
* You are able to reliably sense the flyback pulse from the horizontal-sweep section of the tv set.
* You can lock your computer to the outside world with only a few microseconds of jitter.

So, to use your snuffler, build yourself a sensor to pick off the fly-back pulse, and then clean up the pulse so that it looks like something your computer can understand. Then, use this signal to delay the start of a field. After locking, use some software equalization to minimize the lock transient, and then put down a few blank lines. Then go on to your live display.

Looking at the big picture, 60 times a second something interrupts your main program and says to start a display. After this command, your computer spins its wheels until the next flyback pulse from the snuffler arrives. Then the computer outputs video to the tv set. Then the computer goes back to your main program. How much time is spent on the display determines both the display size and the time left over to run your programs. Shortly, we'll see a 16×64 display that is fully transparent, uses scungy video, and leaves well over half the computer time available for your main program.

BUILDING THE SNUFFLER

The new snuffler circuit is shown in Fig. 2-2, and the construction details of the snuffler coil are shown in Fig. 2-3.

The snuffler coil is made from a length of hookup wire. Use around 40 feet of wire, and hank wind it into a 3-inch diameter loop. Then secure the coils with tape. Finally, the two leads are tightly twisted together and made long enough to get conveniently from tv set to computer. Around 10 feet or so is reasonable.

You put the coil at the lower left rear of your tv set, where it can couple to the flyback transformer in the tv. The coil is then connected to the circuit of Fig. 2-2A. The CMOS Schmitt inverter or gate acts as a high impedance level detector with lots of noise immunity. An input signal above 2.5 volts drives the output *low*. An input signal below this value drives the output *high*. The Schmitt input circuitry provides noise immunity through its *hysteresis* or snap-action. This is just what we need to condition the more-or-less messy flyback pulse.

Debug will be simplest if you use a scope for your initial check-out. View Point A. The flyback peaks should be around five volts high. You adjust the strength with the sensitivity pot and the positioning of the coil on the outside of your tv set. Once you find a good location, hold the coil in place with masking tape. Try to find a position that gives you five volts out with a centered sensitivity pot, when viewed with the usual 10-megohm 10:1 scope probe.

Once the position is nailed down, operation should be noncritical and reliable. If you don't have a scope, use your KIM-1 and a custom program to measure the times between overflow sets. No overflows

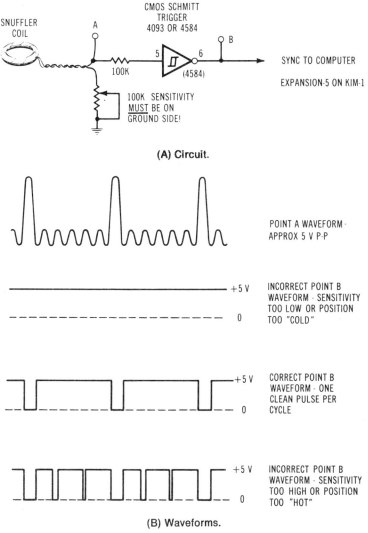

(A) Circuit.

POINT A WAVEFORM -
APPROX 5 V P-P

INCORRECT POINT B
WAVEFORM - SENSITIVITY
TOO LOW OR POSITION
TOO "COLD"

CORRECT POINT B
WAVEFORM - ONE
CLEAN PULSE PER
CYCLE

INCORRECT POINT B
WAVEFORM - SENSITIVITY
TOO HIGH OR POSITION
TOO "HOT"

(B) Waveforms.

Fig. 2-2. Snuffler circuitry.

mean too low a sensitivity, and erratic overflows mean too hot a coil
position or too high a sensitivity setting.

Note that the sensitivity pot MUST go on the ground side of the
snuffler coil. Otherwise, the snuffler coil self-shields and gives you
far too low an output signal.

Your point B waveform should give you one clean output pulse
per input flyback pulse.

START WITH 40 FEET OF SOLID HOOKUP
WIRE. HANK WIND 20 FEET AS 20 TURNS
ON 3 INCH DIAMETER.

SECURE LOOP WITH TAPE. TWIST LEADS
TOGETHER. STRIP ENDS.

TAPE TO TV SET AT LOWER LEFT REAR.
USE OSCILLOSCOPE TO FIND
"LOUDEST" POSITION.

Fig. 2-3. Details of snuffler coil.

A SNUFFLER DEMONSTRATOR

Fig. 2-4 shows a demonstration program that puts a stable raster on the screen for you. It's a handy place to start. It demonstrates the full transparency of the snuffler method. The demo assumes you have the old TVT 6⅝ cheap video system and both PROMs in use.

The snuffler works by interrupting an existing program. Start out with the default "main" program shown starting at 0100.

This particular display will give you a blank raster or else one with a bunch of stripes. Later on, you'll replace the blank raster with the live scan format of your choice.

We use the interval timer on the KIM-1. This gives us an interrupt 60 times a second. This interrupt stops the main program and starts the video display sequence.

The interrupt from the timer branches us to 1780. When we get to 1780, we wait for the next flyback pulse from the snuffler. After the snuffler sync arrives, we put down 20 or so blank scans. Most often, we can get by with far fewer prescan blanks than this, but 20 is a good choice for very stable displays. These blanks are put down in step 178C.

The live scans follow and are set down by 1796. The stripes you'll get correspond to the first dot row of whatever happens to be in display memory locations 0014 to 003F. Since this is a demonstration, all we are interested in is showing a stable live scan area separate from the rest of your program and the blank scans. Later, of course, you'll replace the live scan with something useful.

After the live scans, we output a vertical sync pulse and set the timer to get us a new interrupt as needed next time around. Be sure to jumper your timer to the IRQ line (APP15 to EXP4). Once your timer is set, the interrupt is released, and the computer returns to the main program.

The sum of the prescan blanks, the live scan lines, and the timer value must add up to a stationary hum bar at 60 hertz when the tv horizontal hold is at its best setting. Be sure to follow the detailed notes in Fig. 2-4. Your program is working when you have a stationary display and 50% throughput.

Your Turn:

Add interlace and line lock to the snuffler.

Interlace is fairly easy to add. Just change the timer value and the vertical sync position for each field of your frame. Combine N scan lines and a late V sync pulse on one field with N + 1 scan lines and an early V sync pulse on the second field. See details on this in Chapter 2 of *The Cheap Video Cookbook.* Shortly, we will look at an alternative to full interlace that gives you much higher throughput on fancy displays.

Line lock will be tricky. The advantages of line lock are that it eliminates the timer and gives you a stationary hum bar. But some-

---

μP—6502	Start—JMP 0100	Program Space—1780–17A6
System—KIM−1 +	Stop—Reset	(39 words)
TVT 6⅝ +		IRQ—1780
Snuffler		(17FE–80; 17FF–17)

This program puts a raster on the screen with about 50% throughput. It uses the TVT 6⅝ with PROMs 658-KD8 and 658-KS64, along with a snuffler circuit applying flyback timing routed to the overflow set pin. The display is fully transparent.

Use the following as a default main program to be interrupted:

0100	A9 10	LDA	#10	Start IRQ Timer first cycle
0102	8d 0F 17	STA	170F	continued
0105	58	CLI		Clear Interrupt flag
0106	4C 05 01	JMP	0105	Loop till scan interrupts

Scan Program:

1780	b8	CLV		Wait for flyback pulse
1781	50 FE	BVC	1781	continued

(Continued on next page)

Fig. 2-4. Snuffler demonstration program for TVT 6⅝.

```
1783    50 00          BVC    1705     Equalize 2 or 3 µs as needed
1785    20 10 60       JSR    6010     Equalize even µs as needed

1788    A2 14          LDX    #14      Set # of initial blank scans
178A    70 00          BVS    178C     Equalize 3 µs
178C    20 10 60       JSR    6010     /////INITIAL BLANK SCANS/////
178F    CA             DEX             One less blank scan

1790    d0 FA          BNE    178C     Done with blank scans?
1792    A2 80          LDX    #80      Set # of live scans
1794    70 00          BVS    1796     Equalize 3 µs
1796    20 14 70       JSR    7010     /////LIVE SCANS//////////////

1799    EA             NOP             Equalize 4 µs
179A    EA             NOP                        continued
179b    CA             DEX             One less live scan
179C    d0 F8          BNE    1796     Done with live scans?

179E    A9 71          LDA    #71      Set IRQ timer for rest of field
17A0    8d 0E 17       STA    170E                continued
17A3    AD 00 E0       LDA    E000     Output vertical sync pulse
17A6    40             RTI             Return to main program
```

Notes:

TVT $6^5/8$ must be connected and both the Scan (658-KS64) and Decode (658-KD8) PROMs must be in circuit to run. Snuffler must input clean flyback pulses to SEO pin (#38-6502; EXP5-KIM-1)

IRQ vector must be set to 1780 (17FE 80; 17FF 17)

Normal settings: Module A or D; OFF; +; 64; FAST

Step 1783 provides even or odd equalization as needed. Use 50 for 2 µs and 70 for 3 µs. Step 1786 provides multiples of 2 microseconds for equalization. These two steps together set the tv horizontal lock transient.

Step 1789 picks the number of prescan blanks. Step 1793 picks the number of live scan lines. Step 179F picks the remaining field time after scan, in roughly one-scan increments. These three values interact. **Their sum must be adjusted for a stationary hum bar at the tv's best hold setting.**

Tv set hold control must be adjusted for a near vertical presentation. Display consists of first dot row of characters stored in 0014 to 003F. In a real application, any desired scan format can replace this demonstration scan.

Fig. 2-4. Cont'd. Snuffler demonstration

Tv horizontal frequency approximately 15625 Hz; vertical approximately 60 Hz. Live scan time 64 µs. Live scan lines 128. Hold control may need to be retouched every 30 minutes or so.

KIM interval timer must be jumpered to IRQ line.
    (APP-15 to EXP-4).

Flowchart:

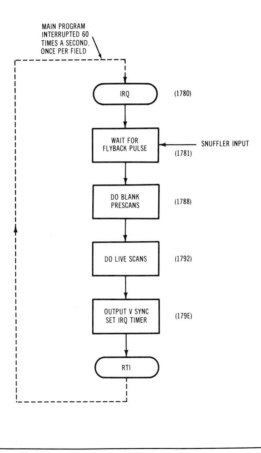

program for TVT 6⅝.

how you have to lock the horizontal frequency to the line as well. Otherwise you will get vertical jitter of your characters.

The obvious source of line lock is a sine wave from the power supply that is filtered and routed through a CMOS Schmitt gate something like we did with the snuffler. But this may jitter too much unless it is further cleaned up with a phase-locked loop or something else workable.

Here are a few unexplored possibilities for line lock:

* Use a clean 60-hertz line signal to speed up or slow down the microprocessor clock slightly.

—or—

* After your live scan time, put down some blank scans that can pull the tv set's sync, speeding up or slowing things down as needed for lock.

—or—

* Make the characters so big that one line of jitter isn't annoying.

Line lock really isn't needed, but it would be very elegant to provide, particularly if you can do it for 20 cents or less.

ALTERNATE-FIELD SNUFFLING

Here is an even more dastardly trick you can play on your tv set. Suppose we use the snuffler and scungy video for one field and then keep the whole next field blank. We would have 30 frames per second. Each frame would have one live field and one blank field at the usual 60-hertz rate. A stunt like this will dramatically raise the throughput, since the computer is free to do what it pleases well over half the time, even with a super-fancy display.

Alternate-field snuffling is an interesting way to up the throughput and is essentially free. All it takes is a change of a few software words in the scan program. Disadvantages we can expect are less brightness, more flicker, and potentially less stability. But on the tv I tested, the results are more than good enough, and you can get a 16 × 64 display with over 50% throughput and full transparency.

To try this on the demonstration program of Fig. 2-4, make the following patches:

1789	19	(This throws in a few extra prescan blank lines to hit exactly 30 hertz)
179F	17	(This picks a longer timer delay)
17A1	0F	(This puts timer in 1024 μs mode)

The best way to find out if alternate-field snuffling works is to try it and see. The tv set has to lock with every *second* vertical sync pulse, but this doesn't seem to be any problem at all. The flicker seems comparable to what you get using double stuffing, maybe a little worse. As usual, watch your contrast and brightness settings. While there are obviously "better" ways to get a video display than alternate-field snuffling, its ridiculously low cost for high throughput and full transparency makes it a useful option for your cheap-video bag of tricks.

THE BEST OF BOTH WORLDS

What happens when we *combine* scungy video and the snuffler? Well, we get extremely flexible, low-cost video displays with full transparency and high computer throughput. Let's look at two examples. First, we will take the 1 × 32 scungy video "bottom line" display and put it in the snuffler demonstrator. Then we'll look at a 16 × 64 video display using your TVT 6⅝ to get high throughput and full transparency.

Transparent 1 × 32

Our 1 × 32 example will use the snuffler and break mapping. This takes only a bare KIM-1 and a TVT 6⅝ without any Scan or Decode PROMs. We'll use the existing RAM in your KIM-1 for the display map. The display you get is fully transparent and leaves over 75% throughput remaining for your main programs.

While a single-line short display might not seem like much in the way of performance, note that we are adding around $7 worth of parts to a bare-bones KIM-1, getting video out of it, and transparently running other programs at the same time. This is a dramatic example of what scungy video can do for you.

Our scan program and its flowchart are shown in Fig. 2-5. Except for one or two details, the program combines our existing scungy, nontransparent display of Fig. 1-14 with the snuffler demonstrator of Fig. 2-4. Rather than use the Scan PROM 658-KS64 as we did on the snuffler demonstrator, we'll use existing RAM inside the KIM-1 to save needing a custom part.

Another detail that is involved in combining scungy video with the snuffler concerns the IRQ line. It looks like we have to ask our interrupt to do *two* different things. First, it has to get us to the scan program sixty times a second when our main program is interrupted by a timer. Secondly, since we are using break mapping in this example, we also will need the IRQ vector to point at the display map for us every time we want to put down a dot row.

To get the IRQ line to do two different things, just change the IRQ vector locations (17FE low and 17FF high) twice during the scan program. When we begin the scan program, we anticipate that this IRQ vector will be needed later for the break mapping and change it. Then, when we are done with our live scans, we change

```
µP—6502                    Start—JMP 0100      Displayed—0380–039F
System—KIM-1 +             Stop—RST            Program Space—0200–0250
         Scungy Video                          Display Map Space—1780–179F
                                               IRQ—0200 for scan program
                                                    1780 for display map
```

This program uses the bare-bones KIM and a TVT 6⁵/₈ without any PROMs to give a video display with a total system cost as low as $7. The circuits of Figs. 1-10A, 1-11, 1-12, and 2-2A are used. Throughput is above 75% with total transparency.

Use the following as a default main program to be interrupted:

```
0100   A9 00        LDA   #00      Set IRQ to Scan Program
0102   8d FE 17      STA   17FE        continued
0105   A9 02        LDA   #02          continued
0107   8d FF 17      STA   17FF        continued

010A   A9 10        LDA   #10      Start IRQ timer 1st scan
010C   8d 0F 17      STA   170F        continued
010F   58           CLI            Clear IRQ flag
0110   4C 10 01      JMP   0110     Loop till scan interrupts
```

Scan Program:

```
IRQ
entry→ 0200   b8           CLV            Wait for flyback pulse
       0201   50 FE        BVC   0201        continued
       0203   EE 00 17      INC   1700     Start V Sync pulse
       0206   A0 70        LDY   #70      Equalize lock transient

       0208   88           DEY               continued
       0209   d0 Fd        BNE   0208        continued
       020b   A9 80        LDA   #80      Change IRQ to Display Map
       020d   8d FE 17      STA   17FE        continued

       0210   A9 17        LDA   #17          continued
       0212   8d FF 17      STA   17FF        continued
       0215   A9 FF        LDA   #FF      Make sure A port is output
       0217   8d 01 17      STA   1701        continued

       021A   A2 30        LDX   #30      Set # of prescan blanks
       021C   A9 00        LDA   #00      End V Sync pulse
       021E   8d 00 17      STA   1700        continued
       0221   EA           NOP            Equalize 2 microseconds
```

Fig. 2-5. 1 × 32 transparent

0222	EE 00 17	INC	1700	Output H sync pulse only
0225	CE 00 17	DEC	1700	continued
0228	A9 10	LDA	#10	Set # of dots per character
022A	A0 09	LDY	#05	Delay for blank scan
022C	88	DEY		continued
022d	d0 Fd	BNE	022C	continued
022F	CA	DEX		One less prescan blank line
0230	d0 EF	BNE	0221	Do another prescan blank line?
0232	F0 00	BEQ	0234	Equalize 3 microseconds
0234	EE 00 17	INC	1700	H sync pulse; advance row counter
0237	EE 00 17	INC	1700	continued
023A	00 EA	BRK		/////SCAN MICROINSTRUCTION////
023C	Cd 00 17	CMP	1700	Is this the last dot row?
023F	d0 F3	BNE	0234	No, do another dot row
0241	A9 0C	LDA	#0C	Set timer for next field
0243	8d 0F 17	STA	170F	continued
0246	A9 00	LDA	#00	Change IRQ to Scan Program
0248	8d FE 17	STA	17FE	continued
024b	A9 02	LDA	#02	continued
024d	8d FF 17	STA	17FF	continued
0250	40	RTI		Return to main program

Scan Microinstruction:

1780	A0 A0 A0 A0 A0 A0 A0 A0	
1788	A0 A0 A0 A0 A0 A0 A0 A0	
1790	A0 A0 A0 A0 A0 A0 A0 A0	(Fifteen LDY A0's followed
1798	A0 A0 A0 A0 A0 A0 40 40	by one RTI)

Notes:

Main user program must initialize IRQ to 0200 and start timer.

Timer must be jumpered to IRQ line (APP-15 to EXP-4). TVT $6^5/8$ must have IC1, 2, and 3 removed per Fig. 1-11. Fig. 1-12 output stage recommended. Snuffler circuit of Fig. 2-2A also must be used.

Remaining transparent throughput is approximately 75%.

The sum of locations 0206 (transient and V sync width), 021b (# of prescan blanks), and 0242 (timer field delay) must add to 16.7 milliseconds for a stationary hum bar.

Horizontal frequency 14,925 Hz. Vertical frequency with properly set horizontal hold control 60.0 hertz; stationary hum bar.

(Continued on next page)

TVT 6⅝ scan program.

the IRQ vector back again to point to the start of the scan program we will need on the next field.

The IRQ vector must point to 0200 for the scan program and to 1780 to get us on the display map. We'll assume your main program does not need or use the IRQ vector; if it does, some more straightening-out should solve things for you.

For your first test, use a "default" main program starting as shown at 0100. Set your IRQ vector to make sure it points to 0200, and then whap the timer once to generate the interrupt for the first display field. End up with a continuous loop as shown in the jump-to-yourself trap in 0110.

Flowchart:

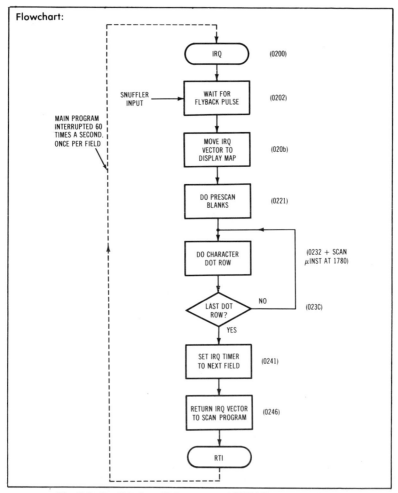

Fig. 2-5. Cont'd. 1 × 32 transparent TVT 6⅝ scan program.

When the first timer interrupt arrives, we vector to 0200 and start our *Scan Program*. The first thing we do is spin our wheels until the flyback pulse from the snuffler arrives by way of the SO input. Then, we start a vertical sync pulse and use the *width* of this pulse to adjust our lock transient to something acceptable. The width of the vertical sync pulse is not at all critical to the tv set; anything over 150 microseconds should do, with the upper limit set by what you want in the way of throughput.

From this point in our scan program, we go on to move our IRQ vector to point at the display map (1780). We next make sure the parallel A port is an output, pick the number of prescan blank lines, and then end the vertical sync pulse. Remember that our vertical and horizontal sync pulses both appear on the same A port line—the difference in time duration is the only difference between the two pulses.

Our prescan blanks follow. This lets things even out before we attempt to put down any character dots. The prescan blanks also give us some space between the V sync pulse and the message, letting the message end up near the top of the screen and down far enough to be legible.

To do a blank scan, we increment and then decrement parallel port A. This gives us a horizontal sync pulse without advancing the row counter lines. After the sync pulse is complete, we use the Y register as a timer to stall for the rest of the line, ending up with a total line time of 67 microseconds.

These operations repeat over and over until enough prescan blank lines are put down. Our program uses 48 prescan blanks, enough to make the display stable and move it well onto the screen, but not enough to really cut into the throughput.

Once our prescan blanks are finished, we go on to put down our live character rows. We do this by incrementing the A port twice. This gives us a horizontal sync pulse *and* advances the row dot counter. After the sync pulse is finished, we do a break-mapped interrupt to the display map. The display map is located at 1780. It gives us a scan microinstruction that advances our program counter one count per microsecond for 32 consecutive microseconds. This is the action we need to let a line of 32 character dots go out the upstream tap and appear as video.

After a scan microinstruction is complete, we test the A port to see if we have finished the bottom dot row. This is done in step 023C. If we have not done all seven dot rows needed for a line of characters, we repeat the process and pick up a new row of dots. When we are finished, we go on to complete the scan program.

When the complete characters are put down, the scan program sets the timer for the next field and moves the IRQ vector back to point at 0200, where we will start the next field. When all is done, we exit to our main program.

The entire process of locking to the snuffler, putting down the prescan blanks, doing the live scans, and exiting takes a few milliseconds. For the rest of the time, your main program is free to run, and the tv set goes on putting down blank lines without any horizontal sync input. The process repeats 60 times a second to give you a stationary display. Around 75% of the time is available for your main program to run.

Your Turn:

> Show a software vertical position control for your display. Can you move the display down without decreasing the throughput? What is the maximum transparent throughput you can get and still have a stable display?

Some program slots may need adjustment to suit your particular tv. The lock transient and vertical sync width is set by 0207. The number of prescan blanks is controlled by 021b. The time to the next field is set by 0242.

Your time to the next field is a coarse adjustment. No way will you exactly hit a stationary hum bar unless you really luck out. So, use the number of prescan blanks and the vertical sync width to fine tune to a stationary hum bar. There will be some interaction between the *horizontal* hold control and the hum-bar timing. Aim for a stationary hum bar with the most stable display. Your horizontal hold may occasionally need retouching.

16 × 64 or 16 × 40

Let's do either a 16 × 64 or a 16 × 40 transparent display as a final example of something fancy you can do with scungy video. Let's assume you have an old TVT 6⅝ along with its Scan PROM 658-KS64, and a KIM-1 with extra RAM added on. Let's assume you have at least 1K of RAM immediately above the usual, and that decoding K4 on the KIM is still free. If your K4 happens to be in use as part of RAM or PROM space, just work out another decoding scheme. Be sure to remember that your display map is picked by your decoding, and that your display map *must* be outside the display memory upstream tap address space.

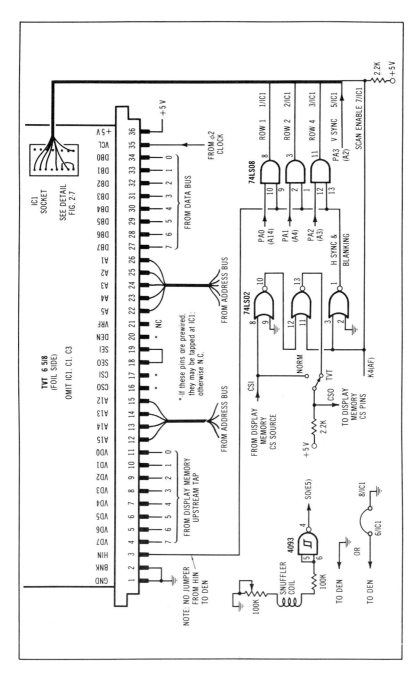

Fig. 2-6. Transparent scungy video circuit for 16 × 40 or 16 × 64 display.

The circuit is shown in Fig. 2-6. The display memory will usually be across the *new* RAM in your system, since a full 1K will be needed for either display format. This, of course, means that your upstream tap also has to go across the new memory, just like we used a tap on the KIM-2 add-on memory in *The Cheap Video Cookbook*.

Your TVT 6⅝ is modified by removing IC1, C1, and C3, and any existing *connector* jumper between HIN and DEN.

Three new ICs are added. One is a CMOS Schmitt trigger for the snuffler, just like we did back in Fig. 2-2A. Two NOR gates are used to combine the display memory chip select *from* the computer with the chip select *from* the TVT and then route this result *to* the display memory. Another NOR gate is used to invert the K4 Scan Enable decoding to give us a signal useful for blanking and the H sync signal. This blanking signal is also routed to three AND gates that move us to "row zero" except during the live portions of the scan.

You can use the empty decode PROM socket IC1 on the TVT 6⅝ to access three row inputs, the vertical sync input, and the Scan Enable. Details on this are shown in Fig. 2-7. *If* you already have your TVT 6⅝ socket prewired, you can also pick off DEN, SEO and SEI at socket IC1. But, for new work, it is best to keep SEI, SEO, and DEN totally off the TVT 6⅝ board.

Note that DEN is now hard-wired to ground. A simple changeover switch between CSO and CSI can be used to pick TVT or normal operation. This switch can be changed at any time without any program bombing problems.

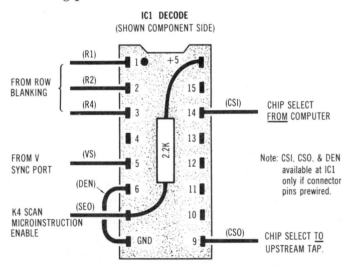

Fig. 2-7. How to access the TVT 6⅝ using the decode PROM socket.

The parallel port assignments appear in Fig. 2-8. Note that rows 1, 2, and 4 occupy the *lowest* lines, while port PA3 serves as a vertical sync pulse source. Horizontal sync and blanking are separately picked off with the NOR gate that inverts the scan decoding K4.

You'll find the scan software in Fig. 2-9. The scan program works by interrupting a main program of your choice. For initial tests, use the default main program shown starting at 0100.

The display memory is on RAM pages 04 through 07. The display map is the K4 decoding space. The scan program resides in 1780 to 17dF. Since this scan program is nonmodifying, it can go elsewhere in RAM, ROM, or PROM.

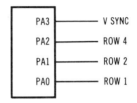

Fig. 2-8. Port assignments for 16 × 64 or 16 × 40 transparent scungy display.

Three locations are reserved on page zero. The display starting address is stored at 0080 (low) and 0081 (high). Location 0082 holds the number of character rows for us. By changing 0082, you can change the number of character rows. This gives one good way to trade off throughput versus the number of characters displayed.

A timer-generated interrupt breaks your main program sixty times a second. The IRQ jumps us to 1780 where we begin our scan program. We first wait for the snuffler pulse to lock us to the tv scanning. Next, we put down a bunch of prescan blanks in steps 178A to 1794, and then set our timer to tell us when the next field is to begin.

To initialize our character scanning, we poke the display memory starting address in 0080 and 0081 and pick the number of rows to be displayed by poking 0082. We then make port A an output and verify that it is on the top blank dot row with no vertical sync. This is done by step 17C6 by clearing the port. The number of vertical dots per character is set by step 17b5 and held in the X register for us.

After initialization, we jump to the character putting-down subroutine starting at 17d6. And here you'll find something new.

Remember that on our early TVT 6⅝ circuits, we had to have code that self-modifies to get by with short code sequences? We could beat this if only we had a jump-to-subroutine-indirect command. This command doesn't seem to exist on the 6502, but we can fake it as shown in Fig. 2-10. You first jump to a "local" subroutine, and then do a "jump indirect" to the scan microinstruction subroutine. The values in 0080 and 0081 tell us where to begin our scan microinstruction.

So, to do a scan microinstruction, we go to a local subroutine that starts at 17d3. We then jump indirect to the display map, using the values in 0080 and 0081 as an address. At the end of the scan micro-

---

μP—6502	Start—JMP 0100	Program Space—1780–17dF
System—KIM-1 +	Stop—Reset	Displayed—0400–0700
Extra Memory+		IRQ—1780 (17FE 80; 17FF 17)
TVT $6^5/8$ +		Reserved Locations:
Snuffler		0080—Display Lo Start
(See Fig. 2-6)		0081—Display Hi Start
		0082—# of Character Rows

This program gives a transparent 16×40 or16×64 video display with high throughput. It uses the circuit of Fig. 2-6. Throughput and line length options are shown in Chart 2-1.

Use the following as a default main program to be interrupted:

	0100	A9 10		LDA	#10	Start IRQ timer first cycle
	0102	8d 0F 17		STA	170F	continued
	0105	58		CLI		Clear interrupt flag
	0106	4C 05 01		JMP	0105	Loop till scan interrupts

Scan Program:

IRQ →	1780	b8		CLV		Wait for flyback pulse
Entry	1781	50 FE		BVC	1781	continued
	1783	A2 01		LDX	#01	Equalize lock transient
	1785	CA		DEX		
	1786	d0 Fd		BNE	1785	continued
	1787	EA		NOP		Continue equalization
	1788	EA		NOP		continued
	1789	EA		NOP		continued
	178A	A2 14		LDX	#14	Set # of prescan blanks
	178C	20 18 10		JSR	1018	/////Prescan Blanks/////
	178F	48		PHA		Equalize 11 μs
	1790	68		PLA		continued
	1791	EA		NOP		continued
	1792	EA		NOP		continued
	1793	CA		DEX		One less prescan blank
	1794	d0 F6		BNE	178C	Done?
	1796	A9 EF		LDA	#DF	Set timer for next field
	1798	8d 0E 17		STA	170E	continued
	179b	EA		NOP		Equalize 6 μs
	179C	EA		NOP		continued

Fig. 2-9. 16 × 40 or 16 × 64 transparent TVT 6⅝

instruction, the RTS command undoes the original JSR, and we go back to the scan program.

	179d	F0 00	BNE	179F	continued
	179F	A9 18	LDA	#18	Set Display Memory Start Low
	17A1	85 80	STA	0080	continued
	17A3	A9 10	LDA	#10	Set Display Memory Start High
	17A5	85 81	STA	0081	continued
	17A7	A9 10	LDA	#10	Set # of character rows
	17A9	85 82	STA	0082	continued
	17Ab	A9 FF	LDA	#FF	Make A ports all outputs
	17Ad	8d 01 17	STA	1701	continued
	17b0	20 38 10	JSR	1038	///Blank Equalizing Scan////
	17b3	d0 00	BNE	17b5	Equalize 3 µs
	17b5	A2 08	LDX	#08	Set # of dots per character
	17b7	20 d6 17	JSR	17d6	GO TO LIVE CHARACTER SCANS
	17bA	18	CLC		Find next row start address
	17bb	A5 80	LDA	0080	continued
	17bd	69 40	ADC	#40	continued
	17bF	85 80	STA	0080	continued
	17C1	90 0d	BCC	17d0	Page Overflow?
	17C3	EE 81 00	INC	0081	Yes, fix
	17C6	A9 00	LDA	#00	Clear A port (row 0, no sync)
	17C8	8d 00 17	STA	1700	continued
	17Cb	C6 82	DEC	82	One less character row
	17Cd	d0 E1	BNE	17b0	Done with last character row?
Exit ←	17CF	40	RTI		Yes, exit to main program
to main					
program	17d0	EA	NOP		No Page Overflow Bypass
	17d1	90 F3	BCC	17C6	continued
	17d3	6C 80 00	JMP	(0080)	((Jump to scan instruction))
	17d6	20 d3 17	JSR	17d3	////Live Character Scans////
	17d9	EE 00 17	INC	1700	Advance character dot row
	17dC	CA	DEX		Done with last dot row?
	17dd	d0 F7	BNE	17d6	No, do another dot row
	17dF	60	RTS		Yes, exit character subroutine

Notes:

IRQ Vector must be set to 1780 (17FE 80; 17FF 17)

Normal Settings: Module A or D; OFF; +; 64; FAST; No IC1

KIM Interval Timer must be jumpered to the IRQ line (APP-15 to EXP-4)

scungy video scan program using snuffler.

(continued on next page)

Flowchart:

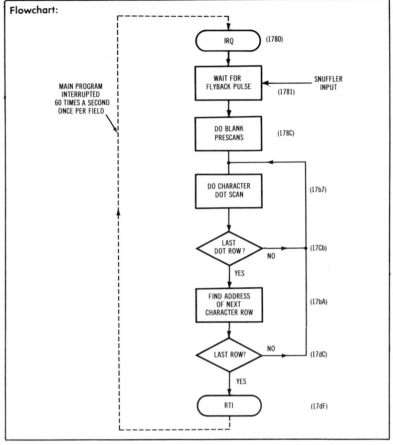

Fig. 2-9. Cont'd. 16 × 40 or 16 × 64 transparent TVT 6⅝ scungy video scan program using snuffler.

The advantage of this route is that all your code can be in ROM or PROM, except for two page zero locations. The disadvantages are a few extra code words and the extra 5 microseconds it takes to do a scan microinstruction due to the JSR indirect command. But, there's enough room in the 16 × 40 display to still let you run on a normal horizontal frequency, and the 16 × 64 will need a much lower horizontal frequency anyway, so the extra 5 microseconds is something you can live with either way.

To put down a row of dots, we do a jump to a local subroutine that does a jump indirect to the display map. The display map gives us our scan microinstruction to put down a dot row and then returns us to the scan program.

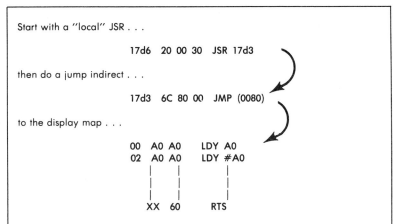

```
Start with a "local" JSR . . .

                    17d6   20 00 30   JSR 17d3

then do a jump indirect . . .

                    17d3   6C 80 00   JMP (0080)

to the display map . . .

                    00   A0 A0    LDY A0
                    02   A0 A0    LDY #A0
                         |  |         |
                         |  |         |
                         |  |         |
                    XX   60       RTS
```

which does the usual scan microinstruction. In this example, a "00" in 0080 and an "07" in 0081 point us to 0700.

Step 0300 does a jump indirect to the display map and scan microinstruction starting address held in 0080 (low) and 0081 (high). This "JSR indirect" approach takes 5 code words and 5 microseconds extra.

Fig. 2-10. How to "fake" a "JSR indirect" op code on a 6502.

After a dot row is complete, step 17d9 advances us to the next dot row, and 17dC checks to see if this is the final dot row. If our character row is not finished, we keep repeating scan microinstructions until we are done. Then we exit our character putting-down subroutine to get back to our main scan program.

To get a new row of characters, we take the old starting address in 0080 and 0081 and add hex 40 to it in step 17bd. We restore the new value in 0080 and then check for a page overflow. If the page overflows, the carry bit sets, and we increment 0081 high address in step 17C3. If no page overflow happens, we use 17d0 and 17d1 to take up exactly as much time as if an overflow happened, and then go on.

When we have the starting address for a new line, we make sure the A port is on the top row, and then we go on to our dot row subroutine again at 17d6.

At the end of the last dot row of the last character row, we do an RTI and exit to the main program at 17CF.

That's quite a bit of nesting for one program. Fig. 2-11 should clarify the action. Your main program is interrupted 60 times a second by the *scan program*. When the scan program wants a character row, it subroutine calls the *live character scans* sequence. When the live character scans coding wants to put down a single row of dots,

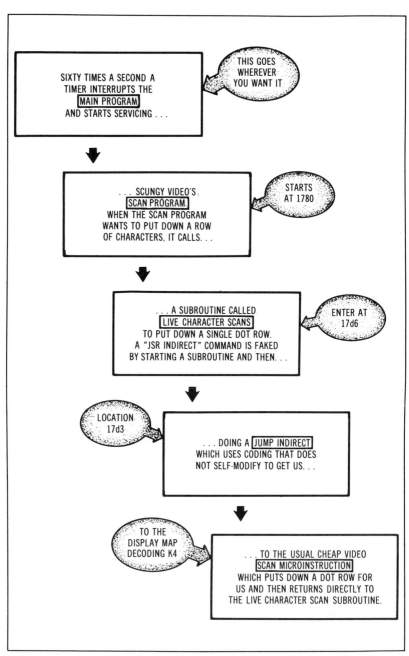

Fig. 2-11. Software nesting for 16 × 40 or 16 × 64 transparent scungy video.

it calls a local subroutine which does a jump indirect to the scan microinstruction on the display map.

Things unwind just the way they built up. A finished scan microinstruction subroutine returns to the live character scans subroutine. When live character scans is finished, it exits to the scan program. When the scan program is finished, it releases the interrupt, and the main program picks up where it left off. For the rest of the frame, the main program does its thing, and the tv goes ahead putting down blank lines without any external sync.

Your Turn:

Show how the vertical sync pulse gets output in the right place. *Hint:* What happens if you set the V POS control far too low?

If you understand where our vertical sync pulse comes from, you have a good start at understanding this circuit and program. Note that our vertical sync pulse takes *zero* lines of code. This is a pretty fair example of efficient coding.

Chart 2-1 shows some options for this circuit and scan program. You can go 16 × 64 or 16 × 40 and either do so at the usual 60 times a second or use alternate-field snuffling with 30 frames a second, just by changing seven words of code.

The 16 × 40 programs run at nearly normal horizontal hold settings, while the 16 × 64s take the much lower hold settings and are

Chart 2-1. Options for 16 × 40 or 16 × 64 Transparent Scungy Video Display

Step	Function	16 × 40 Normal	16 × 40 High Throughput	16 × 64 Normal	16 × 64 High Throughput
178b	Prescan Blanks	14	17	14	17
1797	Timer Fine	EF	1F	E4	1E
1799	Timer Coarse	0E	0F	0E	0F
178d	Blank Scan Length	18	18	00	00
1761	Equalizing Scan Length	38	38	20	20
17A0	Live Scan Length	18	18	00	00
1784	Lock Transient Adj	01?	01?	24?	24?
	Throughput	37%	67%	10%	52%
	H Line Time	66 µs	66 µs	90 µs	90 µs
	Hold Setting	Normal	Normal	Low	Low
	Field Rate	60/s	30/s	60/s	30/s

limited to small-screen black-and-white sets, as we detailed in *The Cheap Video Cookbook*.

Throughput will be much higher for the alternate-field snuffling options, but the display may not be as bright and may flicker somewhat. Question marks are shown for the *lock transient adjust* values, since these may vary for your particular set. Pick whatever gives you a straight and stable display.

Note that one of the options gives you a 16×64 display with 50% throughput.

SOME PERSPECTIVE

What good is scungy video and where can we use it? Scungy video is useful to put video onto bottom-line systems where cost is very important and you want to hold both dollars and circuit complexity to the absolute minimum. There is no reason why scungy video cannot be added to most popular microprocessors for $10 or less for your *total* hardware costs of video display.

For fancier systems, we are better off replacing the snuffler with fixed field and line timing. This timing can be generated totally by the CPU, it can be done with a fancy controller chip, or a counter or sync fill-in method can be used instead. Details on some of these methods were shown in the last chapter of *The Cheap Video Cookbook*.

Note that many of the features of scungy video are easy to apply to older cheap video systems. The elimination of bipolar PROMs, the freeing up of large bunches of address space, the elimination of self-modifying code, and so on—all of these ideas are easy to use on fancy video displays at very low cost. Which of these concepts can you put to use?

CHAPTER 3

Custom Characters

How would you like to display *any* character or graphics chunk of your choosing on a cheap video system? If you add a pick-your-own feature to your cheap video system, you could:

* Deliver a message in Swahili with Icelandic subtitles.
* Do printed circuit layouts and logic diagrams right on the screen.
* Directly display music scores or game pieces with minimum software.
* Provide lower-case character shapes and descenders your way rather than someone else's.
* Add one or two special symbols to a stock symbol or character set.
* Eliminate completely any delivery hassles over "stock" character generators.

Now, there is one sure-fire way to do all this. And it takes nothing in the way of special hardware. You can simply use a high-resolution graphics display with an enormous RAM, along with bunches of software. With this brute-force attack, you get the symbols out of a file somewhere and remap them onto a screen memory.

The advantages of brute-force, hi-res graphics are extreme flexibility and the elimination of special hardware. The disadvantages are needing lots of RAM, very long software sequences, and volatility that destroys the characters or symbols on power-down or if a program goes astray.

Do we have any other alternatives to brute-force, hi-res graphics or stock character generators?

Suppose you could build your own character generator and put up to 256 characters of your choice into it. You then simply replace the stock character generator with your new custom one. The new one has the characters or symbols you designed into it. As these characters are called, they appear on the screen.

The characters are nonvolatile and available when you need them. You can call any character with a single software word from a single memory slot, rather than needing the eight or more words called for by brute-force methods.

Even better, a character can be *anything*. It can be a graphics symbol or a chunk of a graphics symbol. You can put these symbols side-by-side or top-to-bottom to build up complete displays. For instance, a pair of symbols could be used to do a music staff with an 8 × 16 bit resolution. Or a symbol quad could give you a 16 × 16 chess piece.

It turns out there is an integrated circuit beast called a 2716 EPROM, short for *Erasable and Programmable Read Only Memory*. You get an EPROM empty, and then you fill it with your choice of ones and zeros in any pattern you like. If you make a mistake or change your mind, you simply erase the EPROM by shining strong ultraviolet light through a window in the top of the EPROM. This erases everything, and you can refill the EPROM with your choice of new material.

You can reprogram as often as you care to. Once you get something you like, you replace the existing character generator with your new EPROM, and your special symbols or whatever are on the air. A new adaptor module, somewhat similar to module "A" of the TVT 6⅝, is needed to change the pinouts around.

There are lots of advantages of using an EPROM as a character generator on a cheap video system:

* You have total control over the character and chunk set.
* Characters, chunks, or groups of chunks can be called with a single software word, dramatically minimizing display memory RAM.
* The characters and chunks are nonvolatile, always there and ready to use.
* The entire personality of your video system can be changed by changing a single integrated circuit.

The disadvantages of EPROMs are that they may cost more than character generators and that a hardware change is needed for a different type of display.

Let's explore using an EPROM as a character generator replacement. We'll first look at EPROMs and then build a simple *Module*

"*E*" adaptor for your TVT 6⅝. We'll find out that the EPROM route is so attractive that you may never want to ever again use a stock character generator. From there, we'll go on to next chapter's design example that lets you do a sophisticated music display *directly* on your minimum KIM-1.

What we show you should easily work out on other systems and other graphics displays.

EPROMs AS CHARACTER GENERATORS

A character generator is a read only memory. An EPROM is a read only memory. The 2716 EPROM is bigger and faster than most character generators. So, simply by rethinking and relabeling things, you ought to be able to use either one to generate characters or graphics symbols. Fig. 3-1 compares the two methods.

In Fig. 3-1A, we use a commercial character generator. There are six or seven input lines that accept ASCII coding. These are our "what-character-do-you-want" input lines. There are also three or four input lines that accept row timing information. These serve as our "what-row-of-dots-are-we-working-on" inputs.

The number of input lines changes with the features offered in any character generator. If you have only 64 characters, then you need only six ASCII input lines. If you are generating characters only 7 or 8 dots high, then you need only the three row commands called R1, R2, and R4. But, if you want 12 or 16 dot rows per character, you have to have a fourth row command called R8. These taller formats give you better lower-case descenders but take fancier timing. They also put fewer characters vertically on the screen, or else take more throughput to put the same number of characters down.

For each and every possible combination of inputs, a row of dots is output. These output dots are routed to a video shift register for conversion to serial video. Output dots may be five, seven, or eight in number. This depends on whether you are working with 5×7 characters, 7×9 characters, or fancy graphics chunks. The 5×7 character has the lowest bandwidth and the simplest timing.

At any rate, if you take away all the fancy input names and callouts, a character generator is nothing but a read only memory with 9 to 11 inputs and 5 to 8 outputs. Since the 2716 EPROM has 11 inputs and 8 outputs ($2K \times 8$), it can replace most any character generator you may want to use.

You can get many different formats out of a 2716. At the extremes, you could get a single character out that was 8 bits wide and 2048 bits high. Or, you could get out 2048 different characters, all one bit high by eight bits wide.

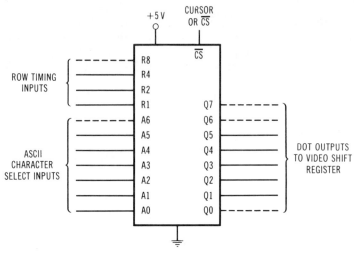

(A) Stock character generator.

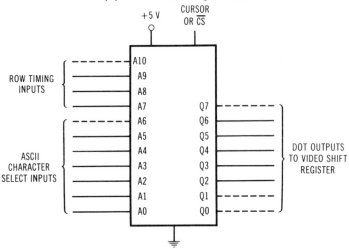

(B) EPROM used as character generator.

Fig. 3-1. If you replace a character generator with an EPROM, you gain complete control over the characters and graphics symbols.

These extremes are seldom useful. Most often, we would be more interested in reasonable combinations of input words and output dots. Several of these format options are shown in Fig. 3-2.

In Fig. 3-2A, we use 8 character select inputs and 3 row select inputs. This gives you 256 *different* characters. Each character is 8 bits wide by 8 bits high in an 8 × 8 matrix. Most often, the cursor is stored as one of these 256 characters. Since we have used all eight

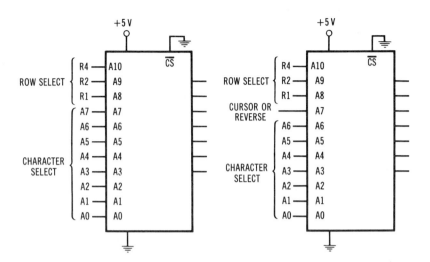

(A) 256 characters, 8 × 8 dot matrix.

(B) 128 characters, 8 × 8 dot matrix, cursor or reverse video.

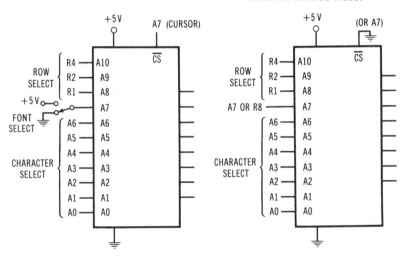

(C) Two fonts of 128 characters each, 8 × 8 dot matrix.

(D) 128 characters, 8 × 16 dot matrix.

Fig. 3-2. Some format options for 2K × 8 EPROM character generators.

input lines available to us on a data bus to pick characters, there is no input bit left for the cursor. So, the cursor becomes a stored character instead.

We have eight output lines. If we want only five, six, or seven of these, we simply output blanks on the unused lines, or else leave them unconnected. Outputting blanks is the better choice, as it gives us compatibility with graphics outputs that may need all eight lines.

In Fig. 3-2B, we get 128 characters, each an 8 × 8 dot matrix. This frees up data bus line A7. We can then use A7 as a software controlled cursor, or we can use it to reverse selected characters, giving us black characters on a white background, or vice versa. To do these options, you make one half of the words inside the EPROM the cursor symbol, or you make one half of the words inside the complement of the other half.

In Fig. 3-2C, we get two fonts or graphics groups of 128 characters each. This lets you pick either font with a jumper or a switch, and still lets you use data bus line A7 as a cursor. This time, A7 forces the outputs high at the chip select input, giving you all white boxes. With some simple extra hardware, you can pick up the winking "jail" type cursor like we did on the TVT 6⅝ (Fig. 4-3, pp 160-161 of *The Cheap Video Cookbook*).

This combination might be useful to let one chip serve for two different games, or to provide special symbols for two different languages.

In Fig. 3-2D, we get 128 characters again, but this time we can make the characters up to 16 bits high by 8 bits wide. The 8 × 16 format is very useful for graphics chunks, such as are needed in the music system we are going to build. An 8 × 12 font has advantages if you want your display to include lower-case characters with attractive descenders.

Somehow, we have to get four inputs to give us a choice of sixteen rows. We have two ways to do this. We can add a new timing line R8 and always generate the 12 or 16 dot high character we need. This fixes everything to the full height, and frees up line A7 for the cursor.

Or, we can use data bus line A7 to be an "upper or lower chunk" selector. This has two advantages. First, it is directly compatible with the existing TVT 6⅝, and second, it lets you *mix* 8 × 8 and 8 × 16 characters inside the same character generator. This gives you many more characters and incredibly more display flexibility. For instance, you can single or double underline characters, and only those characters with descenders would need double chunks.

By the way, it is a simple matter to provide an extra row command on the TVT 6⅝ if you really want to. Simply rework the decode PROM slightly and add a new wire to reach the unused plug-in module pin 12.

So, as you can see, there are lots of new format options you have when you replace a character generator with an EPROM. Can you think of any more?

GRAPHICS CHUNKS

For alphanumerics, you use each character separately as it comes out of the character generator or EPROM. Blanks for the undots between characters are gotten either by coding in your PROM or by hard-wired inputs on the video serial shift register.

To do graphics type stuff, you usually do *not* want these blanks. Instead, you probably want each symbol to butt up against the next one. The individual chunks then combine to give you a complete picture. Since the TVT 6⅝ video shift register accepts a full 8-bit wide dot word, we can easily do both graphics and alphanumerics interchangeably. The same feature is usually possible but may take lots of hardware modifications in other terminals and displays. This is particularly true if the video shift register is less than the full eight bits long.

Fig. 3-3 shows two ways to put together graphics chunks to get bigger symbols. In Fig. 3-3A, we combine the 8 × 8 upper and lower halves of a G-clef to get a treble music staff. In Fig. 3-3B, we use four adjacent symbols to build a rook for a chess display.

Using graphics subelements like this lets you build up attractive, high-resolution symbols with a minimum of software and RAM storage. For instance, the 16 × 16 chess square has a 256 dot resolution, but it is put on the screen with only four words of storage. A full chess screen takes only 256 RAM locations, compared to the 2048 that would be needed in brute-force, hi-res graphics. The software overhead and access times are also much better when you use the call-from-a-character-generator approach.

USING EPROMs

The 2716 is often a top choice for EPROM use. It was one of the first to use a single +5-volt power supply. It is simple to program and erase. You can program the 2716 in-circuit by changing the voltage on a single pin. The 2716 is an industry standard device with standard pinouts, and it is widely available.

While the 2716 was initially an Intel product, the part is second-sourced by just about every semiconductor house. The usual distributors and suppliers that list in the electronics and hobby com-

---

IMPORTANT NOTE: Do NOT use a *Texas Instruments* 2716! This is an obsolete, oddball, multisupply part. The *Texas Instruments* part that is identical to the industry standard 2716 is called a TMS 2516.

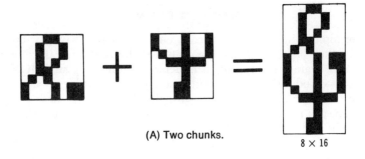

(A) Two chunks.

8 × 16

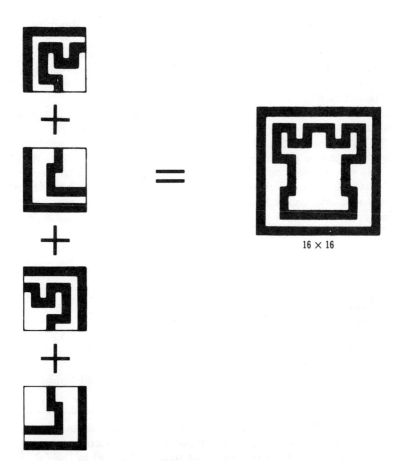

=

16 × 16

(B) Four chunks.

Fig. 3-3. How 8 × 8 graphics chunks may be combined into larger symbols.

puter magazines almost all carry the 2716, so the part is also easy to get. More technical details on the 2716 are shown in Appendix A.

Sources of the 2716 include *American Micro Devices, Fairchild, Intel, Motorola, National, Texas Instruments, American Microsystems, Electronic Arrays, Toshiba, Mostek, Synertek, Hitachi, Mitsubishi,* and *Computer Microsystems.*

Erasing an EPROM

When you get a new EPROM from the factory, all of the bits in all of the locations are supposed to be in the "one" or output *high* state. To make the part useful, you go through an electrical *programming* procedure that changes the ones you *don't* want into zeros. The net result is a *truth table* programmed into the EPROM that meets your needs.

EPROMs are nonvolatile memory. They will hold your truth table forever, with or without power applied. To get back to the "empty" state, an EPROM is erased with high-intensity, *short*-wavelength ultraviolet light. Fig. 3-4 shows a typical 2716. Unlike the usual 24-pin integrated circuits, the 2716 has a transparent lid, usually made as a quartz window. To erase the chip, you shine strong ultraviolet light through the window.

Unfortunately, there is no sane way to erase a single bit. You have to erase the entire 16,384 locations all at once. If you happen to make a programming error that changes a one to a zero, you have to erase everything and start over. If you happen to forget a zero, you can simply reprogram the single bit as needed. Thus, you can put any

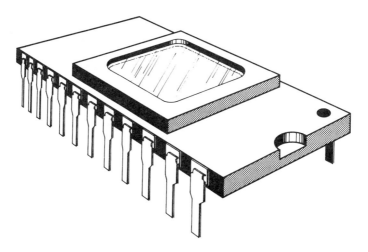

Fig. 3-4. Typical 2716 EPROM.

number of zeros anywhere at any time, but to erase *any* one, the entire chip has to be erased.

Ordinary fluorescent lights and poster "black lights" do not put out short enough wavelengths of uv light to let you erase an EPROM. To erase your EPROM, you can leave it in direct sunlight outside for a week, or you can erase in twelve minutes or so with a suitable lamp specially designed to output *short-wave* ultraviolet energy.

You can buy lamps just for EPROM burning. A few commercial sources of EPROM erasers are listed in Chart 3-1.

Chart 3-1. EPROM Eraser Sources

Electrolabs
Box 6721
Stanford, CA 94305
(415-321-5601)

Information Central
5521 Broadway
Chicago, IL 60640
(312-271-6418)

Ultra Violet Products
5100 Walnut Grove Avenue
San Gabriel, CA 91778
(213-285-3123)

All commercial EPROM erasers have special plastic shields that block uv energy. They usually also have a lockout safety switch that keeps the lamp from lighting when the tray holding the EPROMs is accessible. The EPROM should be held in protective foam during erasure. Several EPROMs can usually be erased at once.

> **IMPORTANT SAFETY NOTE:** Don't EVER look directly at short-wavelength ultraviolet light! Permanent eye damage can result.

Should you have just a single EPROM or two to erase, someone at a local computer club will almost certainly have a lamp you can use. Sometimes rockhound mineral lamps can be used if the filter is removed and the bulb is the short-wavelength type.

It's a good idea to erase all EPROMs completely before programming them, just in case a "new" chip has been preprogrammed.

Programming an EPROM

The 2716 is much easier to program than just about any earlier EPROM. All programming is done with the usual TTL system level signals, except for a single supply pin that gets manually switched to a higher supply voltage.

Chart 3-2 summarizes the rules for reading and programming a 2716 EPROM. There are really only three pins you have to worry about, the *chip enable/program* pin (18), the *output enable* pin (20), and the *programming voltage* pin (21). Here's what they do:

* Pin 18 is the **chip enable.** Hold it *low* to *read* the chip. Hold it *low* to *program* the chip. Only *after* all inputs are stable and *after* you apply the right data, the chip enable is brought high once for exactly 50 milliseconds and then brought low again to complete programming.
* Pin 20 is the **output enable.** Hold it *low* to *read* and *high* to *program.*
* Pin 21 is the **programming voltage** pin. Power it from +5 volts for *read* and from +25 volts for *programming.* The programming +25 volts should be current limited to 40 milliamperes.

So, to read, make VP +5 volts, ground $\overline{OE}$ and ground $\overline{CE}$. To program, make VP +25 volts, make $\overline{OE}$ high, and ground $\overline{CE}$. Then feed the desired address to the address pins and the desired data to be programmed to the output pins. The output pins will act as inputs since $\overline{OE}$ has them floating. After the address is stable, the data is stable, and +25 volts has been applied to VP, bring $\overline{CE}$ high once

Chart 3-2. Three Operating Modes of the 2716

I. To **READ** the memory:

    Apply +5 volts to PROGRAMMING VOLTAGE VP (pin 21).
    Make CHIP ENABLE $\overline{CE}$ (pin 18) **low.**
    Make OUTPUT ENABLE $\overline{OE}$ (pin 20) **low.**

II. To **PROGRAM** the memory:

    Apply +5 volts to PROGRAMMING VOLTAGE VP (pin 21).
    Make CHIP ENABLE $\overline{CE}$ (pin 18) **low.**
    Make OUTPUT ENABLE $\overline{OE}$ (pin 20) **high.**
    Apply +25 volts to PROGRAMMING VOLTAGE VP (pin 21).
    Then — select the correct address and apply the data
        word to be programmed to the **output** pins.
        Then bring CHIP ENABLE $\overline{CE}$ **high** once for exactly
        50 milliseconds. Then return $\overline{CE}$ **low.**
    Bring VP back to +5 volts when finished.

III. To **DESELECT** the memory (standby):

    Apply +5 volts to PROGRAMMING VOLTAGE VP (pin 21).
    Make CHIP ENABLE $\overline{CE}$ (pin 18) **high.**

for exactly 50 milliseconds. Then return CE low before any address is changed.

All bets are off if you hold CE high during programming or if you apply high VP voltage without putting the usual +5 on the chip first. Be very careful to observe these two rules!

There's no need to program an entire EPROM at once. You can use part of it, and then add to your code later.

In theory, you could program your EPROM with nothing but a bunch of slide switches, two power supplies, and a handy source of 50-millisecond single-shot pulses. But there is obsolutely *no way* you can hand program 16,384 bits of information without a mistake. For EPROMs this large, something saner and more automatic MUST be used.

There are lots of 2716 programmers available. Some of these are expensive stand-alone machines. Many work with older EPROMs and thus are much more complicated than needed for 2716s. Some distributors will program 2716s for you free, at least the first time. Usually they will want the code in some inane form like paper tape or punched cards.

Fig. 3-5 shows a simple, low-cost commercial EPROM programmer that attaches to a KIM-1. Chart 3-3 lists a few sources of reasonably priced programmers. Check recent hobby computer magazine articles for do-it-yourself alternatives to these commercial devices. Programming a 2716 requires almost negligible hardware on top of an existing micro such as a KIM-1.

A simple attachment to convert your KIM-1 into an EPROM programmer is shown in block diagram form in Fig. 3-6. All you need is a CMOS binary counter and a regulated power supply. Parts cost is around $3.

Courtesy Optimal Technology, Inc.

Fig. 3-5. An EPROM programmer that fits a KIM-1 or other microcomputer.

Chart 3-3. EPROM Programmer Sources

Microproducts
1024 Seventeenth Street
Hermosa Beach, CA 90254
(213-374-1673)

Oliver Audio Engineering
676 W. Wilson Avenue
Glendale, CA 91203
(213-240-0080)

Optimal Technology, Inc.
Blue Wood 127
Earlysville, VA 22936
(804-973-5482)

Here's how it works. Eight of the KIM's parallel output ports are used to supply the data for programming. Programming addresses are provided by the binary counter whose length matches the needed 11 address lines.

Four additional parallel I/O lines are also used. CLEAR resets the binary counter if it is brought high. COUNT advances the binary counter when it is driven high and then low again. OUTPUT ENABLE controls the output enable, forcing $\overline{OE}$ high during programming and $\overline{OE}$ low for read or verify. The final CHIP ENABLE line is held low for both read and program, except that, during programming, $\overline{CE}$ is brought high once for exactly 50 milliseconds for every word to be programmed. $\overline{CE}$ is then returned low before any input or voltage changes are made.

Your software is mostly a bunch of timer loops. You first initialize things, resetting the counter, making $\overline{CE}$ low and then $\overline{OE}$ high. Then you manually change the program voltage to +25 volts from a 40-mA current-limited source. You then clock the binary counter to pick the addresses and apply the data to the correct output pins of the 2716. The software times out the positive 50-millisecond chip select time after each desired program address and data is applied.

Most often, you'll get your data out of RAM storage in sequential order as needed. Obviously, you should check this *entire* data table before starting. Since you can make several programming passes, this table needn't be the full 2048 words in size. For instance, you can program 512 words at a time using pages 2 and 3 of a bare KIM-1, and make four passes to complete burning the whole chip.

To do this, adjust your software to let the counter run until it gets to the right address, and only then start applying the 50-millisecond CE high pulses. The whole process takes around two minutes. You can follow programming with a verify check, testing everything to be sure it is correct.

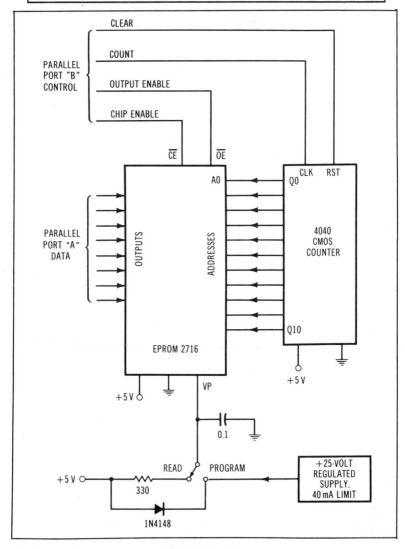

Your Turn:

Show the software needed to program a
2716 EPROM on a KIM-1.

PARALLEL PORT "B" CONTROL

CLEAR

COUNT

OUTPUT ENABLE

CHIP ENABLE

$\overline{CE}$ $\overline{OE}$

A0

PARALLEL PORT "A" DATA

OUTPUTS

ADDRESSES

EPROM 2716

+5 V

VP

CLK   RST

Q0

4040 CMOS COUNTER

Q10

+5 V

0.1

READ   PROGRAM

+5 V

330

1N4148

+25-VOLT REGULATED SUPPLY, 40 mA LIMIT

Fig. 3-6. This circuit and suitable software let you program a 2716 with your KIM-1 microcomputer.

Chances are you can find someone in a local club to burn a single EPROM for you or loan you a programmer. Only, don't expect him to hand load 2048 words of code for you, unless he happens to be a *very* good friend.

Some EPROM Programming Hints

Here are three hints that may save you hours of grief if you do build your own EPROM programmer:

1. If you are using a separate power supply for VP, make the ground connection directly to the EPROM card, and connect the positive supply directly to the 25-volt regulator used for programming. These precautions keep noise off the rest of the computer bus.
2. Make sure there is no way to suddenly discharge a bypass capacitor charged to 25 volts back into the computer's +5-volt bus. The 330-ohm resistor shown in Fig. 3-6 limits discharge current to a safe value. Spiking the power supply on a microcomputer can raise all sorts of havoc.
3. Be sure everything *else* is removed from the parallel ports when you are programming your EPROM. Leaving a keyboard encoder connected, or having a short to ground on, say, PA7, left over from previous cheap video use does the strangest things to your EPROM data.

DESIGNING A CHARACTER SET

Character and graphics dot programs for an EPROM are much easier to design than the usual EPROM stuff, since you can *look* at your results ahead of time, and since there is a one-to-one correspondence between the stored code and the dots that appear on the screen.

Fig. 3-7 shows a form that makes designing characters and graphics simple and orderly.

A typical symbol is shown listed on the form in Fig. 3-8. The address of the character is located in the upper boxes. This is the base *location* in the EPROM where you want the symbol or character to reside. The hex coding for the various dot rows goes on the left. This is the *data* you want stored in your EPROM at the symbol location. Note that there are actually *eight* different data locations, decided by the row code selected. The address code is the *base* address for code 000. We'll see a detailed example of how to use these forms later when we do a music display.

There are several ground rules that you'll want to follow to make your symbols more attractive.

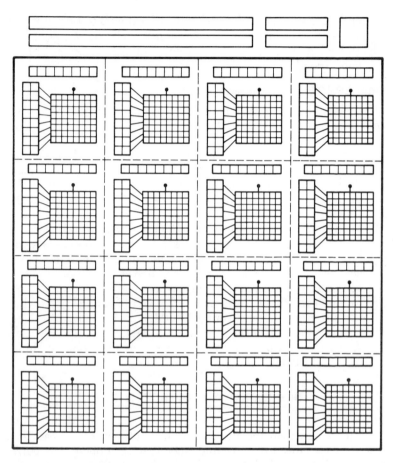

Fig. 3-7. This form helps you design your own EPROM characters or graphics chunks.

* Use the lowest resolution you can. Counting on detail from every last dot may limit your display to quality video monitors. Tv sets may smear adjacent dots together and make the symbols illegible.
* Rely on the overall, dominant, or bulk shape to give the viewer all he needs to know to tell the character or symbol from the others.
* High resolution vertically is much easier go get than high resolution horizontally.
* Make all the symbols look like they "belong" together. Use the same style, height, and the same general overall font "vibes."
* Test to be sure adjacent characters or chunks work well to-

gether, particularly in graphics where subelements have to combine in building a larger image.

* Check your results on an actual video display. There are enough differences between pen-on-paper and electrons-on-screen that on-screen testing is a must.

Actually, we'll be violating our "low resolution" rule on the music display, just to show you the potential of hi-res graphics. As a result, our music will look best on a monitor and may not look too good on a cheap to average-quality tv set.

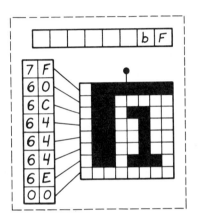

Fig. 3-8. Example of how to use EPROM character design block.

You can *emulate* your EPROM character generator symbols on just about any microcomputer or terminal that lets you put chunks or dots on a screen. Fig. 3-9 shows a way to put large symbols on an Apple II that makes it easy to create and change your symbols. This program is good to show how well graphics subelements will work together.

To use the program, you type R, L, U, or D to move the cursor to a desired square. "1" lights the square; "0" puts it out. "X" clears everything. A red cursor appears briefly after every keystroke, so if you watch for this indicator you can always know where you are on the screen.

Be sure to do some sort of character emulation ahead of time. For example, the music display presented in the following chapter had to be redone several times in order to make the notes and the note dots look good together.

We'll pick up more details on designing characters and symbols in just a bit. But, first, let's go on and build up a simple adaptor that lets you plug an EPROM into your TVT 6⅝ or other video display system.

This BASIC program is useful to design your own characters and graphic shapes. It's especially good to see how the symbols will work and how they will look on a screen.

The program is shown for an Apple II.

```
10    REM: CHARACTER GENERATOR SYMBOL EMULATOR FOR APPLE II
11    REM: U=UP D=DOWN L=LEFT R=RIGHT X=CLEAR 1=LIGHT 0=DARK
12    REM: CR=CURSOR RUN+CR=START CTRL C=STOP

15    DIM A$(10): X=0: Y=0

20    INPUT A$
30            IF A$="R" THEN GOSUB 300
40            IF A$="L" THEN GOSUB 400
50            IF A$="U" THEN GOSUB 500
60            IF A$="D" THEN GOSUB 600
70            IF A$="X" THEN GOSUB 700
80            IF A$="1" THEN GOSUB 800
90            IF A$="0" THEN GOSUB 900

100           Z=SCRN(X,Y):COLOR=1: PLOT X,Y
110           FOR N=1 TO 125: NEXT N
120           COLOR=Z: PLOT X,Y

130           GO TO 20

200   REM: 20 GETS COMMAND; 30-90 PICK SUBROUTINE; 100-120 BRIEFLY
210   REM: FLASHES CURSOR; 130 LOOPS FOR NEXT COMMAND. SUBS FOLLOW:

300   IF X<40 THEN X=X+1: RETURN
400   IF X >0 THEN X=X-1: RETURN
500   IF Y >0 THEN Y=Y-1: RETURN
600   IF Y <40 THEN Y=Y+1: RETURN
700   GR: RETURN
800   COLOR=6: PLOT X,Y: RETURN
900   COLOR=0: PLOT X,Y: RETURN
1000  END
```

Notes:

To use the program, type RUN followed by a RETURN. "U," "D," "R," and "L" move the cursor around. The cursor briefly appears in red after each activity. "1" lights the cursed position, while "0" puts it out. A RETURN must follow each command. CTRL-C stops the program. The display is a very large dot matrix 40 × 40 array.

Fig. 3-9. Character generator symbol emulator.

BUILDING EPROM ADAPTOR MODULE "E"

All you really need to put a 2716 EPROM onto a TVT 6⅝ or other computer or terminal that has 2513 style pinouts is a simple adaptor to rearrange the pins. Fig. 3-10 shows details on a *Custom Programmed EPROM Module "E."*

You can make this adapter from a 24-pin DIP carrier, a small PC card, a 24-pin socket, and five jumpers. The adaptor rearranges the pins so that a 2716 looks like the "enhanced" 2513 pinout arrangement we used on the TVT 6⅝.

On the 2716, programming pin VP is permanently held at +5 volts. The output enable and chip enable pins are tied together and routed to the module's cursor input. The cursor input is held grounded by the OFF position of the cursor switch. With the cursor switch in the CON position, a "1" on upstream tap line VD7 will flash the "jail" cursor as is done on modules "A" and "D." Module pin 12 is not used, while pin 1 provides a permanent ground to the serial input of the video shift register.

Construction might go something like this:

( ) Carefully inspect the circuit board for opens, solder bridges, etc. Try tinning one of the pads on the board. If there is any problem with easy solder adhesion, carefully clean all areas to be soldered with an ordinary pink eraser. Avoid handling the board, as this will make soldering harder.

( ) Place the PC board bare side up with the notch at the upper left. Insert a 24-pin IC socket in the 24 holes at the upper right. Put any code notch indicating pin one of the socket at the *top* of the board. Bend all the socket pins flat against the foil and solder in place. *Important note:* Be sure the socket goes in the upper righthand corner.

( ) Insert a bare wire jumper in the bottom two holes and solder in place (Fig. 3-10C).

( ) Insert a bare wire jumper in the two holes just to the left of the socket and solder in place.

( ) Turn the PC board over so that the foil side is up and the notch is at the upper right. Try fitting the 24-pin PC carrier onto the unused and unsoldered 24 foil pads. The jumpers we are going to add in the next four steps are not to interfere with our later mounting of this socket. So, be sure jumper leads are routed "end around" and not through any pads.

( ) Note the pin numbering (Fig. 3-10D). The rightmost column refers to *DIP Carrier* numbers and goes vertically from pin 1 at the top to pin 12 at the bottom. The next column

Custom Programmed

Parts List

1—2716 EPROM, programmed as wanted
1—24 pin DIP socket
1—24 pin DIP carrier
1—Circuit board "E"
2—jumpers, bare, #24 solid wire
3—jumpers, insulated, #24 solid wire
 —solder
 —flux remover
 —protective foam

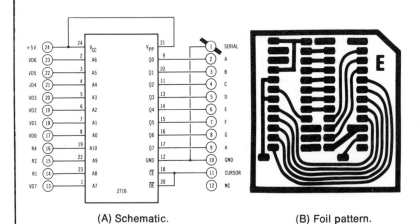

(A) Schematic.   (B) Foil pattern.

Fig. 3-10. Module "E"

E

EPROM Module

How It Works

8-bit character or chunk code is input on pins VD0 through VD7. Corresponding 8-bit dot code appears on outputs A through H. Row inputs R1, R2, and R4 select dot row. Input VD7 can act as cursor, font select, or upper/lower chunk select as desired. CURSOR input is grounded to provide display, made high to float outputs and output all-white box.

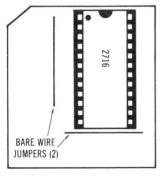

BARE WIRE
JUMPERS (2)

(C) Bare side.

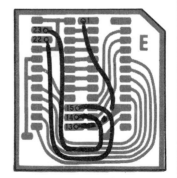

(D) Foil side before mounting
DIP carrier.

Normal Settings: | Cursor OFF; FAST clock; WIDTH set to EIGHT pulses

construction details.

over is the *EPROM Socket* and numbers vertically again with pin 1 at the top and pin 12 at the bottom. Unlike our earlier modules, *both* the DIP Carrier and the EPROM socket number "clockwise" when viewed from the bottom or foil side.

( ) Study Fig. 3-10D. Put an insulated wire jumper between EPROM socket pin 1 and DIP Carrier pin 13. Route this lead well to the right, leaving the pads at DIP Carrier 14 and DIP Carrier 15 exposed.

( ) Route a fairly long insulated wire jumper from DIP Carrier pin 14 to EPROM socket pin 23. Be sure this wire goes around the bottom and not through the pins. Test your DIP carrier again to make sure it will still fit.

( ) Route a similar insulated wire jumper from DIP Carrier pin 15 to EPROM socket pin 22. Be sure this wire also goes around the bottom and not through the pins.

( ) Neaten the position of these three jumpers, and once again check to make sure the dip carrier will fit.

( ) Check to see how hard it will be to solder your dip carrier in place. Find a suitable small-tipped soldering iron.

( ) Study Fig. 3-11. If you have to, cut one each of the small dual barbs on each pin end of the DIP Carrier as shown. Again, if it will help soldering, file off any flanges or anything else that keeps you from soldering at close range. **Do not file the insulating portion of the carrier down so close that soldering heat can loosen the pins.** Remove only as much material as you have to in order to solder the carrier in place.

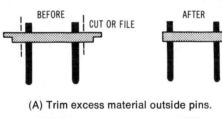

(A) Trim excess material outside pins.

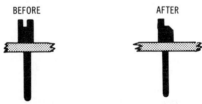

(B) Clip one barb off each pin.

Fig. 3-11. The 24-pin DIP carrier may have to be modified to ease soldering.

( ) Carefully tin each of the remaining 24 pads on the PC board, leaving a nice, even, medium-height bump of solder on each pin.

( ) Tin the pin ends of the dip carrier that are to be soldered to the PC card.

( ) Carefully align the Dip Carrier to the PC board. Then "reflow" solder the pins together. Fig. 3-12 shows how the board will look after the DIP Carrier is in place.

( ) Use a magnifying glass to make sure all pins are in fact soldered and no pins are shorted to adjacent ones.

( ) Clean the board with flux remover or lacquer thinner.

( ) Press the board into a piece of protective foam. Then insert the already programmed 2716 EPROM so that pin 1 is nearest the notched corner.

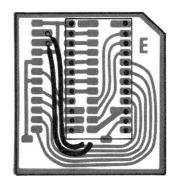

Fig. 3-12. Foil side of Module "E" after reflow soldering DIP carrier.

This completes the assembly of your Module "E." Always store module "E" in protective foam when not in use. If you are using several 2716s, keep them in foam as well.

CHECKOUT

For a quick test, get your TVT 6⅝ up and working with alphanumeric Module A or D and a random character load. Then unplug the alpha module and plug in Module "E." A new random display should result, depending on the program you put in your EPROM.

Your choice of format per Fig. 3-2 decides what you are going to do with lead A7, how your cursor is to be entered, and whether or not you will use a Row 8 line. For most uses, keep the cursor switch in the OFF position to force grounds on the EPROM's enable inputs as needed for a live output.

Any troubles in your display can give you hints as to EPROM programming difficulties. If the eighth output line is always a zero, possibly a hard-wire ground was left on the parallel port during programming, or else the WIDTH pot is giving you nine clocks per load. If the bottom half of all characters is missing, the programmer stopped short of filling the EPROM. If the whole display is blank, but everything else is apparently "alive," you may have an unprogrammed but erased EPROM. Double or funny single characters can usually be traced to incorrect coding on your worksheets, or an error between the worksheet, your RAM loading, and the actual EPROM programming process. Lots of extra dots may mean an incomplete previous erasure.

CHAPTER 4

A Music Display

Let's do a detailed design example to see just how you can use a 2716 EPROM in a custom alphanumeric or graphics display. Fig. 4-1 shows a photo of a music display that has some very fancy features but still runs on a bare-bones KIM-1 or other "minimum" micro.

The features of our music display are listed in Chart 4-1. We have whole, half, quarter, eighth, and sixteenth notes, any of which can be dotted, flatted, sharped, or naturaled. There are lots of measure and line symbols, a few of the more important keys, and four popular tempos. Above-staff notation includes guitar chords, loudness, ties, repeats, and so on. Additional ties and a location pointing cursor can go below the staff.

Chart 4-1. Features of the Music Display

Monotonic, approximately five measures across the screen. Number of lines varies with display and system.
Whole, half, quarter, eighth, and sixteenth notes, any of which can be made sharp, flat, or dotted. Treble low A through high G, or bass equivalent.
Seven different measure symbols, five keys, four tempos.
Treble and bass clefs, rests, repeats.
Guitar chords A–F, sharps, minors, minor sevenths.
Single and double repeats, loudness, diminuendo, crescendo, loudness, slurs, ties.
Full cursor control.
Above-staff, staff, and below-staff space separately accessible.
Expandable and modifiable.

Fig. 4-1. Music display using EPROM character generator.

On a bare-bones KIM-1, there's room for one music line. This gives you around five measures on the screen at once. It's easy to extend this to almost any size display you want, just by adding memory, or going to a slightly larger micro.

Our music display takes either a video monitor or a *very* good tv set for its display. Results may not be too attractive on an ordinary tv set. Only a single note is displayed at a time in any position. We'll see how to add multiple notes later on.

What we'll be looking at is by no means limited to music. The same ideas will work to give you chess pieces, tanks, foreign languages, PC layouts, circuit symbols, or galactic transports. It all depends on your character set and your *display plan*.

THE DISPLAY PLAN

The first step in designing something new in a custom display is to set up an overall *display plan*. Are you going to use alphanumerics only, mixed alphas and graphics, graphics symbols only, or larger graphics symbols that are built up out of combinations of smaller chunks? How many chunks or characters vertically? How many horizontally? Do the chunks always abut, or are there always to be undots between characters? Is everything 8 × 8 or 8 × 16? Or

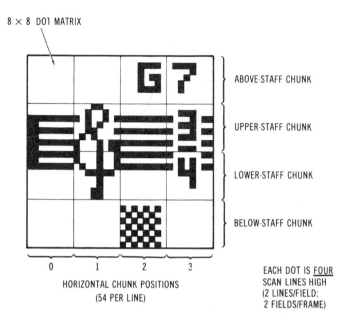

8 × 8 DOT MATRIX

ABOVE-STAFF CHUNK

UPPER-STAFF CHUNK

LOWER-STAFF CHUNK

BELOW-STAFF CHUNK

0   1   2   3

HORIZONTAL CHUNK POSITIONS
(54 PER LINE)

EACH DOT IS <u>FOUR</u>
SCAN LINES HIGH
(2 LINES/FIELD:
2 FIELDS/FRAME)

Fig. 4-2. Four vertical 8 × 8 chunks are used for music display.

are we going to mix matrix sizes to suit the display and still get as many characters or chunk symbols as possible?

Your answers to these questions decide just how you are going to build your custom display. Always start with these basic questions and then work from there.

For a music display, it turns out convenient to use a matrix that is 8 dots wide by 16 dots high for many of the symbols. Fig. 4-2 shows a useful display plan.

We will use a graphics space that is four chunks high by 54 chunks wide. The width is set by the tv or monitor capabilities and is adjustable. This is typically enough space for five or six measures. Our initial plan will be for a single line of music; later you can easily extend things with more memory and different scan software.

We'll make a single dot *four* lines high. To do this, we will use two lines on the first field and two additional lines on the interlaced second field. Anything less than this looks pretty bad.

Our vertical display space is made up of four chunks, the *above-staff* chunk, the *upper staff* chunk, the *lower-staff* chunk, and the *below-staff* chunk. The middle two chunks are paired with software to give us an 8 × 16 dot symbol space. The actual staff lines are somewhat *above* center in this 8 × 16 space, since below-staff notes (treble low A through D) are more common than above-staff ones.

The above-staff chunk gives us room for guitar chords, repeats, diminuendo, ties, and stuff like that. The below-staff chunk will usually be blank, except for a cursor box or possibly some below-staff note ties. This space will also be needed to separate additional lines of music on the screen in fancier displays.

Your staff chunks work as a vertical pair. We will use the convention that the lower chunk will always have an EPROM address of hex 80 more than the upper one, letting us pair chunks easily with software. Thus, two 8×8 chunks will automatically be combined into a single 8×16 symbol. The *location* of our symbol in EPROM will decide whether it gets entered above staff, below staff, or on-staff. We'll see how some simple software sorts things out for us.

Each symbol will be one chunk wide. All on-staff symbols must be arranged to abut each other peacefully. A continuous appearance is gotten by abutting each symbol and having the staff lines exactly align. Usually, we will fill the screen first with an empty staff. The notes will magically "appear" where they belong by replacing the empty staff chunk with a new symbol that has both the staff and the new note on it.

Fig. 4-3 shows the display space we will use if we are on a barebones KIM-1. Most of page two is used as shown. The width of the display is adjusted by changing the starting address to suit the tv or monitor in use. Up to eight music lines can be put on screen with a larger system, just by arranging for a new page of 256 bytes for each line to be displayed, and adding suitable scan and cursor software.

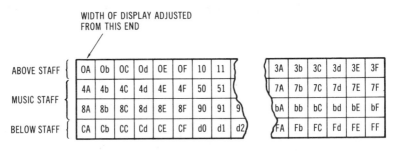

Fig. 4-3. One page of 256 words in a display memory is needed per line of music. Here are typical memory locations used.

A CHARACTER SET

Fig. 4-4 shows the character set we will use. Since you can custom program everything with your EPROM, if you don't like this one, do it your way. This particular set leans heavily toward guitar chording and as a teaching aid for beginning band. While rather fancy, it doesn't let us put more than a single note on a particular location, omits grace notes, and has some compromises in calling for sharps, flats, and naturals. We'll find a sledgehammer way around these limits later, but for now, let's use it as shown.

Each symbol is called by a single word or word pair stored in a display memory. For instance, a hex "3b" will give us the upper half of an eighth note at high "E" on the treble staff.

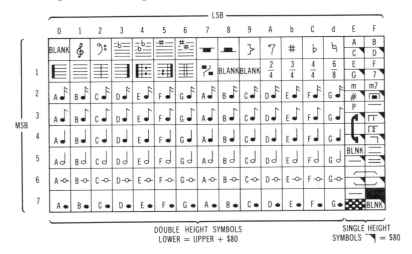

Fig. 4-4. Character set for music display.

Now, if the least significant bit of the word is *d or less,* the symbol will be a double one that needs two chunks. The second chunk address can be found by adding hex 80 to the first, and then storing this value in a suitable display memory location. As we've just seen, a word of "3b" represents the upper-chunk half of eighth-note high "E." The matching lower chunk will have a value of hex (3b + 80) or hex bb. To put a character on the screen, you call for the upper value and store it in the correct display memory location. Then you add hex 80 to this value and store *that* value in the *lower* chunk display memory location that appears immediately below the upper on the screen.

Thus, while only a single word is needed to call an 8 × 16 symbol, *two* words get stored in the proper display memory locations. One of these is the upper chunk, stored as called for. The other is the lower chunk, calculated by adding hex 80 to the upper chunk. While the upper and lower chunk *data* values will be hex 80 apart, the *address* locations in the display memory will be such that they appear immediately above and below each other. Typically, this will be an address difference of decimal 64, or hex 40.

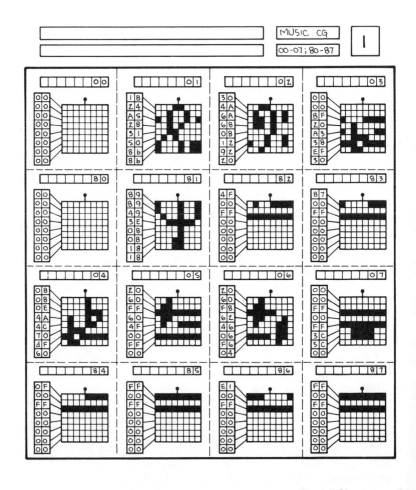

Fig. 4-5 Character set

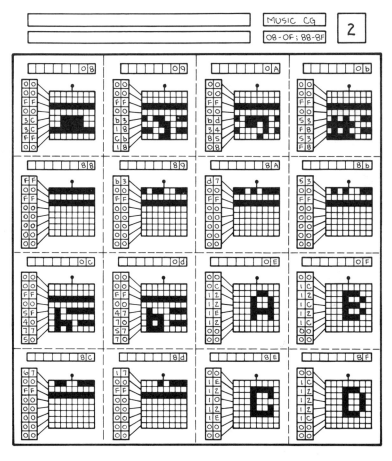

(Continued on next page)

for music display.

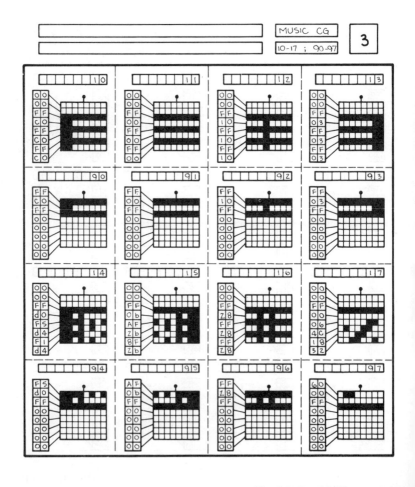

Fig. 4-5. Cont'd. Character set

MUSIC CG

18-1F ; 98-9F

4

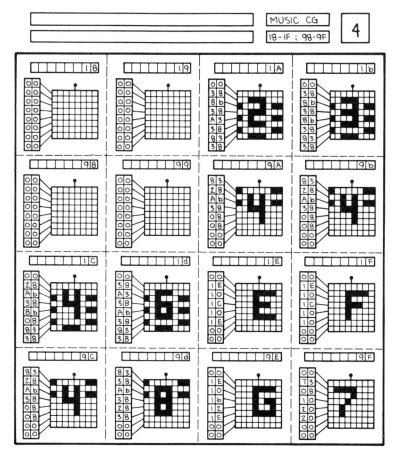

(Continued on next page)

for music display.

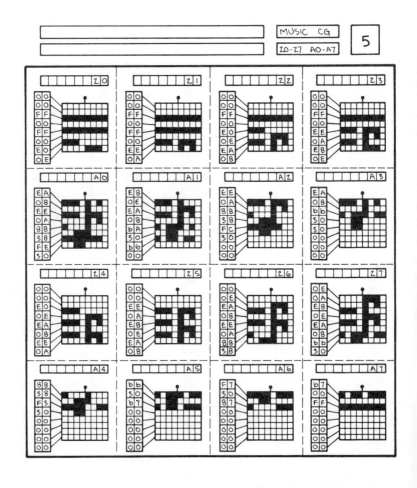

Fig. 4-5. Cont'd. Character set

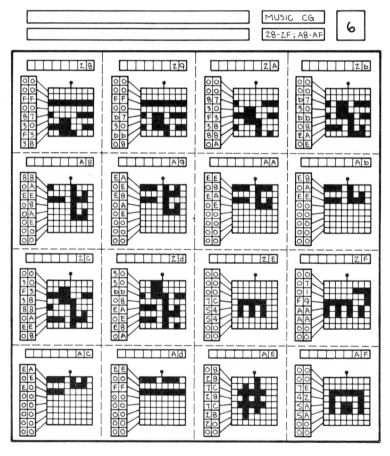

(Continued on next page)

for music display.

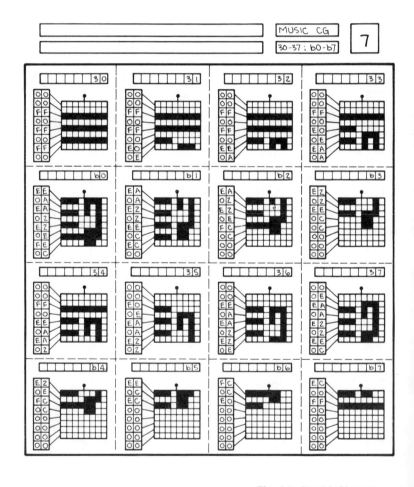

Fig. 4-5. Cont'd. Character set

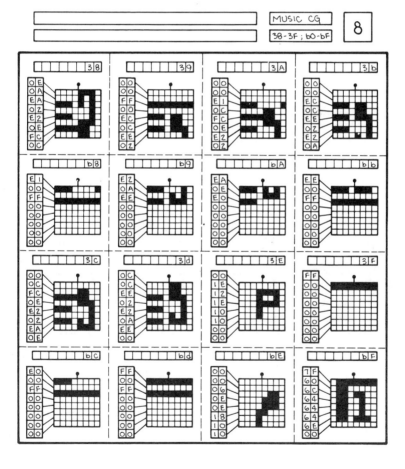

MUSIC CG
38-3F ; b0-bF
8

(Continued on next page)

for music display.

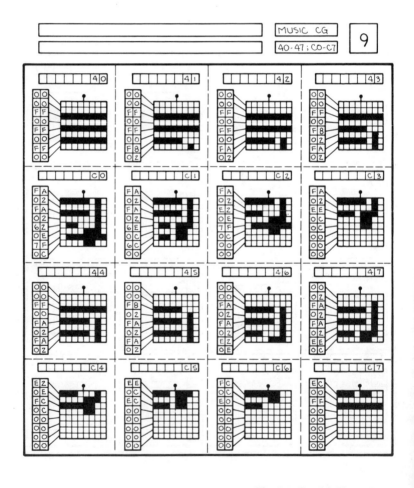

Fig. 4-5. Cont'd. Character set

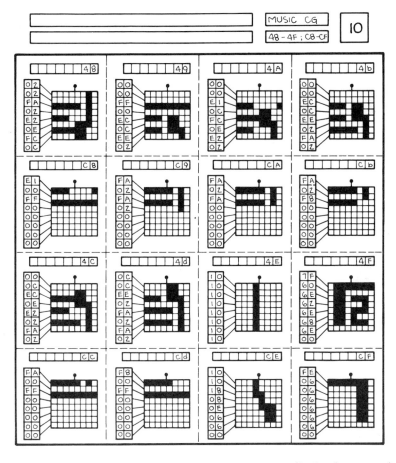

(Continued on next page)

for music display.

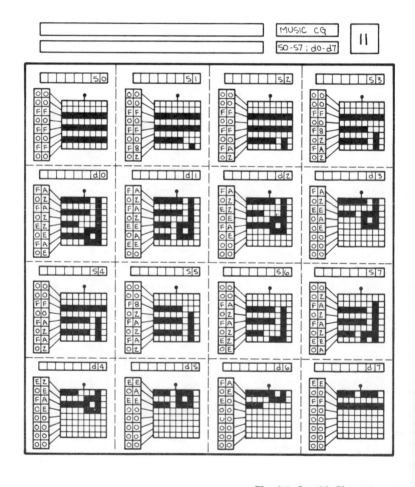

Fig. 4-5. Cont'd. Character set

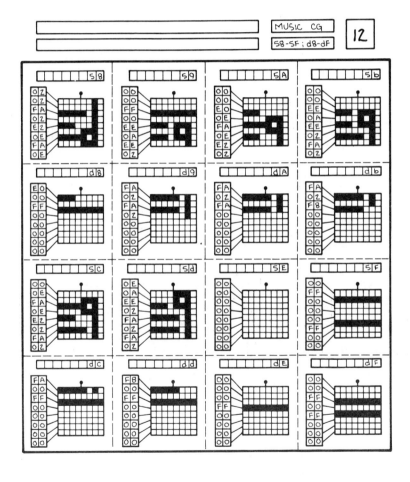

for music display.

(Continued on next page)

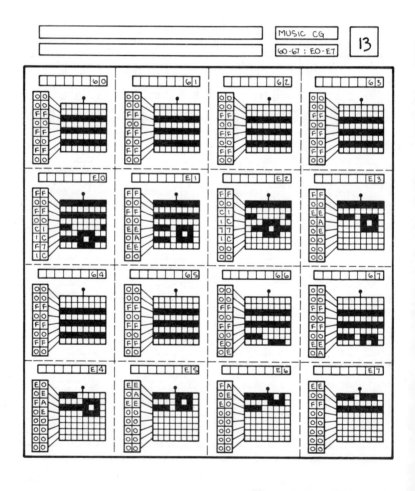

Fig. 4-5. Cont'd. Character set

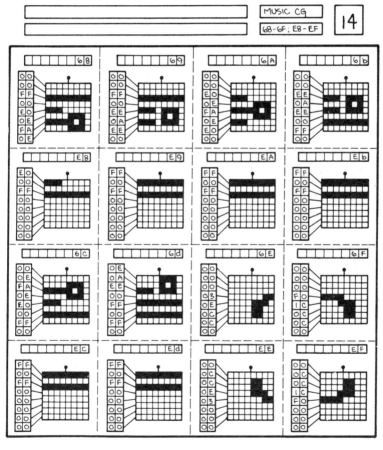

(Continued on next page)

for music display.

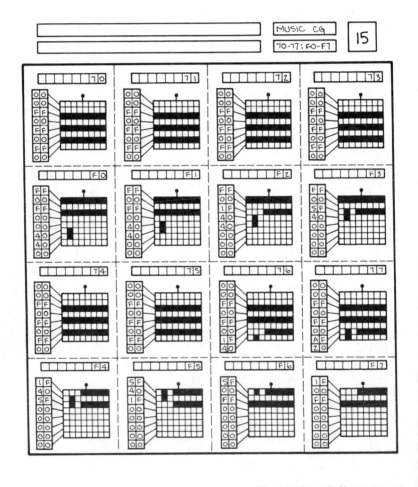

Fig. 4-5. Cont'd. Character set

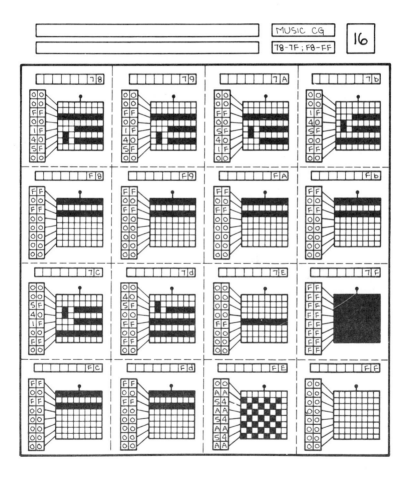

for music display.

```
000   00 18 30 00 08 20 20 00    00 00 00 00 00 00 00 00
010   00 00 00 00 00 00 00 00    00 00 00 00 00 00 00 00
020   00 00 00 00 00 00 00 0E    00 00 00 00 00 30 00 00
030   00 00 00 00 00 00 00 00    0E 00 00 00 00 0C 00 FF

040   00 00 00 00 00 00 00 00    02 00 00 00 00 0C 10 7F
050   00 00 00 00 00 00 00 00    02 00 00 00 00 0E 00 00
060   00 00 00 00 00 00 00 00    00 00 00 00 00 0E 00 00
070   00 00 00 00 00 00 00 00    00 00 00 00 00 00 00 FF

080   00 89 4F 87 0F FF E1 FF    FF b3 d7 53 67 17 00 00
090   FF FF FF FF F5 AF FF 60    00 00 83 83 83 83 00 00
0A0   EA E8 EE EA 88 bb F7 b7    88 EA EE E8 EA EE 08 00
0b0   EE EA EA E2 E2 EE FC EC    E1 E2 EA EE E0 FF 00 7F

0C0   FA FA FA FA E2 EE FC EC    E1 FA FA FA FA F8 10 FE
0d0   FA FA FA FA E2 EE FA EE    E0 FA FA FA FA F8 00 00
0E0   FF FF FF FF E0 EE FA EE    E0 FF FF FF FF FF 00 00
0F0   FF FF FF FF 1F 5F 5F 1F    FF FF FF FF FF FF 00 00

100   00 24 4A 00 08 60 60 00    00 00 00 00 00 00 0C 1C
110   00 00 00 00 00 00 00 00    00 00 38 38 28 38 1E 1E
120   00 00 00 00 00 00 0E 0A    00 00 00 00 30 30 00 07
130   00 00 00 00 00 00 00 0E    0A 00 00 00 0C 0C 1E 00

140   00 00 00 00 00 00 00 02    02 00 00 00 0C 0C 10 60
150   00 00 00 00 00 00 00 02    02 00 00 00 0E 0A 00 FF
160   00 00 00 00 00 00 00 00    00 00 00 00 0E 0A 00 00
170   00 00 00 00 00 00 00 00    00 00 00 00 00 40 00 FF

180   00 89 00 00 00 00 00 00    00 00 00 00 00 00 1E 1C
190   C0 00 10 03 d0 0b 28 00    00 00 28 28 28 38 1E 78
1A0   08 0E 0A 08 38 30 30 00    0A 0E 08 0A 0E 00 28 00
1b0   0A 0A 02 02 0E 0C 0C 00    00 0A 0E 00 00 00 00 60

1C0   02 02 02 02 0E 0C 0C 00    00 02 02 02 00 00 10 06
1d0   02 02 02 02 0E 0A 0E 00    00 02 02 02 00 00 00 00
1E0   00 00 00 00 0E 0A 0E 00    00 00 00 00 00 00 0C 0C
1F0   00 00 00 00 40 40 00 00    00 00 00 00 00 00 AA 00

200   00 A5 6A 8F 0E FF F8 FF    FF FF FF FF FF FF 12 12
210   FF FF FF FF FF FF FF FF    00 00 8b 8b Ab A3 10 10
220   FF FF FF FF E0 EE EA E8    FF FF 87 b7 F3 bb 00 01
230   FF FF FF FF FF E0 EE EA    EA FF E1 EC FC EE 12 00

240   FF FF FF FF FF F8 FA FA    FA FF E1 EC FC EE 10 6E
250   FF FF FF FF FF F8 FA FA    FA FF E0 EE FA EE 00 00
260   FF FF FF FF FF FF FF FF    FF FF E0 EE FA EE 00 00
270   FF FF FF FF FF FF FF FF    FF FF FF 1F 5F 5F 00 FF

280   00 49 FF FF FF FF FF FF    FF FF FF FF FF FF 12 12
290   FF FF FF FF FF FF FF FF    00 00 Ab Ab Ab Ab 10 08
2A0   EE EA 88 bb F3 b7 87 FF    EE E8 EA EE E0 FF 7C 7E
2b0   EA E2 E2 EE FC EC E0 FF    FF EE E0 FF FF FF 06 6C

2C0   FA FA E2 EE FC EC E0 FF    FF FA FA F8 FF FF 18 06
2d0   FA FA E2 EE FA EE E0 FF    FF FA FA F8 FF FF 00 FF
2E0   FF FF C1 EE FA EE E0 FF    FF FF FF FF FF FF 0C 0C
2F0   FF FF 1F 5F 5F 1F FF FF    FF FF FF FF FF FF 54 00
```

Fig. 4-6. Hex dump

108

300	00	28	68	20	4A	60	62	00	00	00	00	00	00	00	12	1C
310	C0	00	10	03	d0	0b	28	00	00	00	38	38	38	38	1C	1C
320	00	00	00	00	0E	0A	08	0E	00	00	30	30	38	08	7C	F9
330	00	00	00	00	00	0E	0A	0A	02	00	0C	0C	0E	02	1E	00
340	00	00	00	00	00	02	02	02	02	00	0C	0C	0E	02	10	62
350	00	00	00	00	00	02	02	02	02	00	0E	0A	0E	02	00	00
360	00	00	00	00	00	00	00	00	00	00	0E	0A	0E	00	03	F0
370	00	00	00	00	00	00	00	00	00	00	00	40	40	00	00	FF
380	00	3E	00	00	00	00	00	00	00	00	00	00	00	00	10	12
390	00	00	00	00	00	00	00	00	00	00	38	38	38	38	16	10
3A0	0A	08	38	30	30	00	00	00	08	0A	0E	00	00	00	28	42
3b0	02	02	0E	0C	0C	00	00	00	00	00	00	00	00	00	0E	64
3C0	02	02	0E	0C	0C	00	00	00	00	02	00	00	00	00	08	06
3d0	02	02	0E	0A	0E	00	00	00	00	02	00	00	00	00	FF	00
3E0	00	00	1C	0A	0E	00	00	00	00	00	00	00	00	00	0E	1C
3F0	00	00	40	40	00	00	00	00	00	00	00	00	00	00	AA	00
400	00	31	08	A3	4C	4F	46	FF	3C	b3	bd	53	5F	47	1E	12
410	FF	FF	FF	FF	F5	AF	FF	06	00	00	A3	8b	8b	Ab	10	10
420	FF	FF	E0	EE	EA	E8	EE	EA	87	b7	F3	bb	88	EA	54	AA
430	FF	FF	FF	E0	EE	EA	EA	E2	E2	EC	FC	EE	E2	E2	10	00
440	FF	FF	FF	F8	FA	FA	FA	FA	E2	EC	FC	EE	E2	FA	10	6E
450	FF	FF	FF	F8	FA	FA	FA	FA	E2	EE	FA	EE	E2	FA	00	00
460	FF	FF	FF	FF	FF	FF	FF	FF	E0	EE	FA	EE	E0	FF	0E	1C
470	FF	FF	FF	FF	FF	FF	FF	FF	1F	1F	5F	5F	1F	FF	FF	FF
480	00	08	00	00	00	00	00	00	00	00	00	00	00	00	12	12
490	00	00	00	00	00	00	00	00	00	00	08	08	08	28	12	20
4A0	88	bA	FC	30	00	00	00	00	0A	0E	00	00	00	00	7C	5A
4b0	E2	EE	FC	0C	00	00	00	00	00	00	00	00	00	00	0E	64
4C0	62	6E	7F	0C	00	00	00	00	00	00	00	00	00	00	0E	06
4d0	E2	EE	FA	0E	00	00	00	00	00	00	00	00	00	00	00	FF
4E0	C1	EE	77	0E	00	00	00	00	00	00	00	00	00	00	03	F0
4F0	00	40	40	00	00	00	00	00	00	00	00	00	00	00	54	00
500	00	50	12	38	70	00	06	3C	3C	18	34	F8	40	70	12	1C
510	C0	00	10	03	d4	2b	28	4C	00	00	38	38	08	38	1E	10
520	00	00	0E	0A	08	0E	0A	08	30	30	38	08	0A	0E	54	AA
530	00	00	00	0E	0A	0A	02	02	0E	0C	0E	02	02	0A	10	00
540	00	00	00	02	02	02	02	02	0E	0C	0E	02	02	02	10	68
550	00	00	00	02	02	02	02	02	0E	0A	0E	02	02	02	00	FF
560	00	00	00	00	00	00	00	00	0E	0A	0E	00	00	00	0C	0C
570	00	00	00	00	00	00	00	00	40	40	40	00	00	00	00	FF
580	00	08	00	00	00	00	00	00	00	00	00	00	00	00	1E	1C
590	00	00	00	00	00	00	00	00	00	00	08	08	08	38	1E	20
5A0	38	30	30	00	00	00	00	00	0E	00	00	00	00	00	28	5A
5b0	0E	0C	0C	00	00	00	00	00	00	00	00	00	00	00	18	64
5C0	0E	0C	0C	00	00	00	00	00	00	00	00	00	00	00	06	06
5d0	0E	0A	0E	00	00	00	0A	00	00	00	00	00	00	00	00	00
5E0	1C	0A	1C	00	00	00	00	00	00	00	00	00	00	00	00	00
5F0	40	40	00	00	00	00	00	00	00	00	00	00	00	00	AA	00

(Continued on next page)

of music PROM coding.

If the least significant bit of the character code is E or F, then we get single-height chunks that are intended to go above or below the staff lines. These symbols will usually go above staff, except for the blanks, cursor, and possibly some ties that might be needed below staff.

The shape of each note is set up so that it can be dotted. Done this way, the separate dot symbols aren't needed for dotted eighth, dotted quarter, and dotted half. But, only a single sharp, flat, or natural symbol is used for the entire staff. This compromise looks good enough on most notes and saves us EPROM space for more useful things.

You'll find two user-definable notes at hex 18 and 19, and there are tricks you can pull to get more space for even more symbols if you really need them.

600	00	8b	92	EF	dF	FF	F6	3C	FF	Cb	85	53	77	57	00	00
610	FF	FF	FF	FF	F1	8F	FF	18	00	00	83	83	83	83	00	00
620	E0	EE	EA	E8	EE	EA	88	bb	F3	bb	88	EA	EE	E8	00	00
630	FF	E0	EE	EA	EA	E2	E2	EE	FC	EE	E2	E2	EA	EE	00	00
640	FF	F8	FA	FA	FA	FA	E2	EE	FC	EE	E2	FA	FA	FA	10	6E
650	FF	F8	FA	FA	FA	FA	E2	EE	FA	EE	E2	FA	FA	FA	00	00
660	FF	FF	FF	FF	FF	FF	E0	EE	FA	EE	E0	FF	FF	FF	0C	0C
670	FF	FF	FF	FF	FF	FF	1F	AF	5F	5F	1F	FF	FF	FF	00	FF
680	00	18	00	00	00	00	00	00	00	00	00	00	00	00	00	00
690	00	00	00	00	00	00	00	00	00	00	00	00	00	00	00	00
6A0	FE	B6	00	00	00	00	00	00	00	00	00	00	00	00	00	00
6b0	FE	EC	00	00	00	00	00	00	00	00	00	00	00	00	10	6E
6C0	7F	6C	00	00	00	00	00	00	00	00	00	00	00	00	06	06
6d0	FA	EE	00	00	00	00	00	00	00	00	00	00	00	00	00	00
6E0	F7	EE	00	00	00	00	00	00	00	00	00	00	00	00	00	00
6F0	40	00	00	00	00	00	00	00	00	00	00	00	00	00	54	00
700	00	8b	20	30	60	00	04	00	00	18	08	F8	50	70	00	00
710	C0	00	10	03	d4	2b	28	32	00	00	38	38	38	38	00	00
720	0E	0A	08	0E	0A	08	38	30	38	08	0A	0E	08	0A	00	00
730	00	0E	0A	0A	02	02	0E	0C	0C	02	02	0A	0E	00	00	00
740	00	02	02	02	02	02	0E	0C	0C	02	02	02	02	02	10	00
750	00	02	02	02	02	02	0E	0A	0E	02	02	02	02	02	00	00
760	00	00	00	00	00	00	0E	0A	0E	00	00	00	00	00	00	00
770	00	00	00	00	00	00	00	00	00	00	00	00	00	00	00	FF
780	00	18	00	00	00	00	00	00	00	00	00	00	00	00	00	00
790	00	00	00	00	00	00	00	00	00	00	00	00	00	00	00	00
7A0	30	00	00	00	00	00	00	00	00	00	00	00	00	00	00	00
7b0	0C	00	00	00	00	00	00	00	00	00	00	00	00	00	10	00
7C0	0C	00	00	00	00	00	00	00	00	00	00	00	00	00	00	00
7d0	0E	00	00	00	00	00	00	00	00	00	00	00	00	00	00	00
7E0	1C	00	00	00	00	00	00	00	00	00	00	00	00	00	00	00
7F0	00	00	00	00	00	00	00	00	00	00	00	00	00	00	AA	00

Fig. 4-6. Cont'd. Hex dump of music PROM coding.

Once you have your design plan and an overall list of what symbols you want and where you want them to go in EPROM, you can go on to design each symbol or symbol pair using the emulation program and the forms we already have looked at in the last chapter.

Fig. 4-5 shows my selection of the music chunks. This character set includes 32 single-height symbols and 112 double-height ones. A dark square on the form indicates *light* on the screen. On each coding square, the hex value for each successive row appears at the left, while the upper-chunk location in EPROM is shown above the symbol.

Once you have your forms complete, you should double-check the coding. Then go to an emulator of some sort that will show you how well the characters work together.

After you are reasonably sure you have workable symbols and believe your coding is right, you can go on and compile a *truth table* for your EPROM. Fig. 4-6 shows the coding we need, as lifted off the music forms.

To generate your truth table, assume your EPROM coding space is broken into 8 pages of 256 words each. Page 000 is the top dot row. Page 100 is the next row down, and so on down to page 700, which is the bottom dot row. Now, go across your symbol sheet, *a row at a time in address order,* to generate your truth table.

For instance, at location 24, the coding for the sixth dot row is EE. Coding EE then appears at location 24 on page 600, or as entry 624 EE on the truth table.

Note that the EPROM doesn't know about the "add hex 80" pairings of the chunks. Each individual 8 × 8 chunk simply goes into the EPROM truth table in the sequence it comes up. Now, our worksheets show the chunks paired. So, you make *two trips* through the worksheet when you compile your truth table, picking up each location in *sequential address* order.

After your truth table is completed, check it thoroughly. If you don't find any mistakes, this means that you haven't checked it well enough. Then load it into RAM somewhere, and make a tape or disc copy of the truth table for future use. Hand loading 2048 words is a bit painful on the KIM keypad. An easier route is to use a full ASCII keyboard and a loader program similar to the one in Fig. 2-21 in *The Cheap Video Cookbook.* This will shorten your routine by some 2048 keystrokes and is far more pleasant to do.

If you do things right the first time, you will only have to make a full 2048 word entry into your computer once. Then change the existing loading so that you won't have to redo the code over and over again.

As soon as you get a good tape or disc copy, program your EPROM. After programming, you can run a quick check on any old alphanumeric display program. This should give you a random load of bits and pieces of badly jumbled music symbols. To get something more interesting, we have to add some music software.

MUSIC SOFTWARE

As usual, it takes a combination of software and hardware working together to get us a useful result. Now that we have our music symbols safely and permanently in EPROM, we need a SCAN program to put things on the screen for us. We also need some sort of a CURSOR program that decides what symbol goes where.

We'll use *four* scan lines for each dot row of the music symbols, two per interlaced field. This makes things large and easy to read. A typical music display program for your KIM-1 and TVT 6⅝ is shown in Fig. 4-7.

We have once again kept the program in several sections to let you rework things any way you like. Our program sections are the main scan, the keyboard interrupt, the cursor processor, and the keyboard formatter.

The main scan gives us a display of 4 × 56 chunks on an otherwise blank screen, accepting note values from a display memory and putting them on the screen.

The keyboard interrupt is a trick to improve transparency. When a key is pressed, the keyboard interrupt program saves this information until the next vertical blanking time, and spends exactly one horizontal line doing so. This "pseudo-transparent" approach gives a very slight bump when a key is pressed. It eliminates the need for a handshaking flip-flop as was used in Fig. 5-5 of *The Cheap Video Cookbook*.

The cursor processor picks up after each key is pressed. It interprets the key strokes. If a cursor entry was made, this program clears the screen, moves the cursor, or turns the cursor OFF or ON. A single key entry is used for cursor motions.

To enter a music chunk, a hex code pair of key closures must be entered, such as a "3b" for our high E eighth note. If a noncontrol character is fed the cursor processor, it is assumed to be part of a valid hex entry which is passed on to the keyboard format part of the program.

The keyboard formatter is a subprogram of the cursor processor. This program combines two hex keystrokes into one word. It then decides where on the staff the symbol is to go. If needed, the keyboard formatter program finds a matching bottom staff chunk and puts it in place.

The reason for separating the keyboard formatter from the cursor processing is mostly to leave you with an option to pick up a better way to enter note commands. As shown, the program takes a hex two-digit entry from an ASCII keyboard to put a symbol on the screen. You might like to use a BASIC string command, or actually input from a real music keyboard instead. This may take a larger system than a bare KIM. There are all sorts of interesting possibilities, so we've kept this part separate.

Here is a more detailed look at how the Music Display program works:

MAIN SCAN PROGRAM—The scan uses a brute-force program that calls each live line as needed, rather than computing each line's location. This eliminates any self-modifying code and lets you put your music scan into PROM or EPROM if you like. Full interlace is used, with the carry bit representing the interlace even-odd flag.

The program starts by putting down the blank scans (steps 0300-0307) followed by calling the live scans as needed for a single field. Each scan is called *twice* for the two lines per dot per field.

After the live scans are finished, the carry bit is saved on the stack to hold the even-odd field value through any cursor processing. A check for a newly pressed key is made by 03C8. Usually, no new key will be pressed, and the scanning will continue. If a key was pressed, the main scan program jumps to the cursor processing subroutine.

Either way, the carry bit even-odd flag is brought back off the stack in 03d0 and then either an even or an odd field sync processing is done to create the interlace. With a *set* carry, an *early* V sync pulse is put down and *one* scan is *removed* from the next field. With a *clear* carry, a *late* V sync pulse is put down and a normal number of scans is used for the next field. The carry bit is then changed so that the next field reverses the process, picking even field if odd and vice versa.

After some equalization in 03Eb, the program jumps back to 0300 for the next field's blank scans. The process is repeated 60 times a second, putting down 30 pairs of even-odd interlaced fields.

KEYBOARD INTERRUPT—Memory location 00EA is a temporary store. Its seven lower bits hold the ASCII keyboard code of the last pressed key. The eighth bit is a flag that tells us "a key is newly pressed that hasn't been processed yet." If the eighth bit is a zero, there is a new key that needs to be serviced. If it is a one, no attention is needed.

The keyboard interrupt program is a short interrupt sequence beginning at 03F3. When a key is pressed, the scan program is in-

μP—6502
System—KIM-1, TVT $6^5/8$, Music "E" plug-in
Start—JMP 0300
Stop—STOP

Cursor Motions — ERASE—clear screen (CAN)
→—cursor right (HT)
←—cursor left (BS)
↑—cursor ON (VT)
↓—cursor OFF (LF)

ENTER—Hex pairs of music code; cursor disappears between first and second entry.

Displayed — 020A–023F (above staff)
024A–027F (upper staff)
028A–02bF (lower staff)
02CA–02FF (below staff)

Program Space — 0300–03FF (MAIN SCAN program)
1780–17dC (CURSOR program)
0100–0129 (KEYBOARD FORMAT program)

00EA—Keyboard strobe and character
00Eb—Character complete flag

00Ed—Cursor low
00EF—Cursor high (02)

17FE—IRQ low F3
17FF—IRQ high 03

Main Scan Program:

```
START→ 0300  20 d2 62   JSR   6212   Do blank scan
       0303  CA         DEX          One less blank scan
       0304  d0 00      BNE   0306   Equalize 3 μs
       0306  d0 F8      BNE   0300   Last blank scan?

       0308  20 10 62   JSR   6210   Scan Staff + 8
       030b  20 0A 62   JSR   620A      again
       030E  20 0A 72   JSR   720A   Scan Staff + 7
       0311  20 0A 72   JSR   720A      again

       0314  20 0A 82   JSR   820A   Scan Staff + 6
       0317  20 0A 82   JSR   820A      again
       031A  20 0A 92   JSR   920A   Scan Staff + 5
       031d  20 0A 92   JSR   920A      again

       0320  20 0A A2   JSR   A20A   Scan Staff + 4
       0323  20 0A A2   JSR   A20A      again
       0326  20 0A b2   JSR   b20A   Scan Staff + 3
       0329  20 0A b2   JSR   b20A      again
```

Fig. 4-7. A music display program

032C	20 0A C2	JSR	C20A	Scan staff + 2
032F	20 0A C2	JSR	C20A	again
0332	20 0A d2	JSR	d20A	Scan staff + 1
0335	20 0A d2	JSR	d20A	again
0338	20 4A 62	JSR	624A	Scan staff 16
033b	20 4A 62	JSR	624A	again
033E	20 4A 72	JSR	724A	Scan staff 15
0341	20 4A 72	JSR	724A	again
0344	20 4A 82	JSR	824A	Scan staff 14
0347	20 4A 82	JSR	824A	again
034A	20 4A 92	JSR	924A	Scan staff 13
034d	20 4A 92	JSR	924A	again
0350	20 4A A2	JSR	A24A	Scan staff 12
0353	20 4A A2	JSR	A24A	again
0356	20 4A b2	JSR	b24A	Scan staff 11
0359	20 4A b2	JSR	b24A	again
035C	20 4A C2	JSR	C24A	Scan staff 10
035F	20 4A C2	JSR	C24A	again
0362	20 4A d2	JSR	d24A	Scan staff 9
0365	20 4A d2	JSR	d24A	again
0368	20 8A 62	JSR	628A	Scan staff 8
036b	20 8A 62	JSR	628A	again
036E	20 8A 72	JSR	728A	Scan staff 7
0371	20 8A 72	JSR	728A	again
0374	20 8A 82	JSR	828A	Scan staff 6
0377	20 8A 82	JSR	828A	again
037A	20 8A 92	JSR	928A	Scan staff 5
037d	20 8A 92	JSR	928A	again
0380	20 8A A2	JSR	A28A	Scan staff 4
0383	20 8A A2	JSR	A28A	again
0386	20 8A b2	JSR	b28A	Scan staff 3
0389	20 8A b2	JSR	b28A	again
038C	20 8A C2	JSR	C28A	Scan staff 2
038F	20 8A C2	JSR	C28A	again
0392	20 8A d2	JSR	d28A	Scan staff 1
0395	20 8A d2	JSR	d28A	again
0398	20 CA 62	JSR	62CA	Scan staff −1
039b	20 CA 62	JSR	62CA	again
039E	20 CA 72	JSR	72CA	Scan staff −2
03A1	20 CA 72	JSR	72CA	again
03A4	20 CA 82	JSR	82CA	Scan staff −3
03A7	20 CA 82	JSR	82CA	again
03AA	20 CA 92	JSR	92CA	Scan staff −4
03Ad	20 CA 92	JSR	92CA	again
03b0	20 CA A2	JSR	A2CA	Scan staff −5
03b3	20 CA A2	JSR	A2CA	again
03b6	20 CA b2	JSR	b2CA	Scan staff −6
03b9	20 CA b2	JSR	b2CA	again

(Continued on next page)

for the KIM-1 and TVT 6⅝.

```
              03bC  20 CA C2    JSR    C2CA   Scan staff −7
              03bF  20 CA C2    JSR    C2CA     again
              03C2  20 CA d2    JSR    d2CA   Scan staff −8
              03C5  20 CA d2    JSR    d2CA     again

              03C8  08          PHP           Save ILCE carry flag
              03C9  24 EA       BIT    EA     Is a new key pressed?
              03Cb  30 03       BMI    03d0   No, continue
              03Cd  20 80 17    JSR    1780   Yes, process CURSOR JSR

              03d0  28          PLP           Get ILCE carry flag back
              03d1  A2 C4       LDX    #C4    Set # of blank scans
              03d3  90 0C       BCC    03E1   Pick even or odd scan
              03d5  AC 00 EA    LDY    EA00   Output odd field V sync pulse

              03d8  A0 05       LDY    #05    Delay 26 μs
              03dA  88          DEY           continued
              03db  d0 Fd       BNE    03dA   continued
              03dd  CA          DEX           Subtract line for odd field

              03dE  18          CLC           Change to even field
              03dF  90 0A       BCC    03Eb   Bypass even field V sync
              03E1  A0 05       LDY    #05    Delay 26 μs
              03E3  88          DEY           continued

              03E4  d0 Fd       BNE    03E3   continued
              03E6  AC 80 E0    LDY    E080   Output even field V Sync pulse
              03E9  EA          NOP           Equalize 2 μs
              03EA  38          SEC           Change to odd field

              03Eb  A0 03       LDY    #03    Equalize 14 μs
              03Ed  88          DEY           continued
              03EE  d0 Fd       BNE    03Ed   continued
              03F0  4C 00 03    JMP    0300   Go to blank scans

KBD IRQ→03F3  48          PHA           Save accumulator
Entry   03F4  Ad 00 17    LDA    1700   Get key from Keyboard
        03F7  85 EA       STA    EA     Hold character in 00EA
        03F9  A9 20       LDA    #20    Equalize timing

        03Fb  4A          LSR           continued
        03FC  d0 Fd       BNE    03Fb   continued
        03FE  68          PLA           Restore accumulator
        03FF  40          RTI           Return to main scan
```

Notes:

To test main scan without keyboard entry, defeat IRQ (00F1 04) and store 80 in the keyboard strobe (00EA 80)

To test main scan with keyboard entry, use 1780 60, and set IRQ vector to 03F3 (17FE F3; 17FF 03).

To eliminate any white parts of the nondisplay area, connect blanking input BNK to DEN (test point HR) instead of to ground. Another route to a clean background is to put the scan program *outside* the memory with the upstream tap.

Fig. 4-7. Cont'd. A music display

Cursor Processing Program:

ENTER →	1780	A9 02	LDA	#02	Set cursor to page two
VIA JSR	1782	85 EE	STA	EE	continued
	1784	A5 Ed	LDA	Ed	Set cursor above staff
	1786	29 3F	AND	#3F	continued
	1788	85 Ed	STA	Ed	continued
	178A	A9 80	LDA	#80	Erase KP strobe flag
	178C	05 EA	ORA	EA	continued
	178E	85 EA	STA	EA	continued
	1790	A0 C0	LDY	C0	Erase old cursor
	1792	A9 00	LDA	#00	continued
	1794	91 Ed	STA	(Ed,Y)	continued
	1796	A5 EA	LDA	EA	Read keyboard
	1798	C9 9F	CMP	#9F	Is key a CTRL command?
	179A	90 03	BCC	179F	yes, move cursor
	179C	4C 00 01	JMP	0100	no, go to keyboard format
	179F	C9 98	CMP	#98	Clear screen?
	17A1	F0 13	BEQ	17b6	yes, go clear screen
	17A3	C9 8A	CMP	#8A	Cursor off?
	17A5	F0 0E	BEQ	17b5	yes, RTS without cursor
	17A7	C9 89	CMP	#89	Cursor right?
	17A9	F0 1b	BEQ	17C6	yes, move cursor right
	17Ab	C9 88	CMP	#88	Backspace cursor?
	17Ad	F0 22	BEQ	17d1	yes, go backspace cursor
	17AF	A0 C0	LDY	#C0	Replace cursor
	17b1	A9 FE	LDA	#FE	continued
	17b3	91 Ed	STA	(Ed),Y	continued
	17b5	60	RTS		Return to main scan

Cursor Processing Sequences:

17b6	A9 00	LDA	#00	CLEAR SCREEN//////////
17b8	85 Ed	STA	Ed	home cursor
17bA	A8	TAY		reset index
17bb	91 Ed	STA	(Ed),y	store blank
17bd	C8	INY		next position
17bE	d0 Fb	BNE	17bb	repeat till end of screen
17C0	A9 0d	LDA	#0d	home cursor
17C2	85 Ed	STA	Ed	continued
17C4	10 E9	BPL	17AF	exit to main cursor program
17C6	A9 3d	LDA	#3d	CURSOR RIGHT//////////
17C8	C5 Ed	CMP	Ed	right end of screen?
17CA	90 02	BCC	17CE	yes, ignore
17CC	E6 Ed	INC	Ed	no, move right one
17CE	4C AF 17	JMP	17AF	exit to main cursor program
17d1	A9 0d	LDA	#0d	CURSOR LEFT///////////////
17d3	C5 Ed	CMP	#Ed	left end of screen?
17d5	b0 02	BCS	17d9	yes, ignore
17d7	C6 Ed	DED	Ed	no, move left one
17d9	4C AF 17	JMP	17AF	exit to main cursor program

(Continued on next page)

program for the KIM-1 and TVT 6⅝.

To test this portion of the cursor and the main scan program independent of the keyboard formatting, use 179C 60.

Keyboard Format Program:

```
0100   A5 EA      LDA    EA       Get keystroke
0102   C9 C0      CMP    #C0      Is it A–F?
0104   90 02      BCC    0108     no, continue
0106   69 08      ADC    #08      yes, correct code

0108   85 EA      STA    EA       replace corrected hex code
010A   24 Eb      BIT    Eb       1st or second keystroke?
010C   30 07      BMI    0115     go enter if second
010E   A5 EA      LDA    EA       get 1st keystroke

0110   09 80      ORA    #80          and erase keyflag
0112   85 Eb      STA    Eb           and hold for 2nd keystroke
0114   60         RTS             Return to await 2nd keystroke
0115   26 Eb      ROL    Eb       Shift 1st keystroke to upper byte

0117   26 Eb      ROL    Eb           continued
0119   26 Eb      ROL    Eb           continued
011b   26 Eb      ROL    Eb           continued
011d   A9 F0      LDA    #F0      Clear lower byte 1st keystroke

011F   25 Eb      AND    Eb           continued
0121   85 Eb      STA    Eb           continued
0123   A5 EA      LDA    EA       Get 2nd keystroke
0125   29 0F      AND    #0F          clear upper byte 2nd keystroke

0127   05 Eb      ORA    Eb       Combine upper and lower bytes
0129   A0 00      LDY    #00      Clear keystroke flag
012b   84 Eb      STY    Eb           continued
012d   A8         TAY             Save character

012E   29 0F      AND    #0F      Is this above staff character?
0130   C9 0E      CMP    #0E          If so, go to above staff entry
0132   b0 0E      BCS    01 2         continued
0134   98         TYA             Get character back

0135   A0 40      LDY    #40      Set cursor to upper staff
0137   91 Ed      STA    (Ed),Y  Store upper staff character
0139   69 80      ADC    #80      Calculate matching lower staff
013b   A0 80      LDY    #80      Set cursor to lower staff

013d   91 Ed      STA    (Ed),Y  Store lower staff character
013F   4C C6 17   JMP    17C6     And return to cursor program
0142   98         TYA             Get character back
0143   A0 00      LDY    #00      Set cursor above staff

0145   91 Ed      STA    (Ed),Y  Store above staff character
0147   4C C6 17                   And return to cursor program
```

Fig. 4-7. Cont'd. A music display

Main Scan Flowchart:

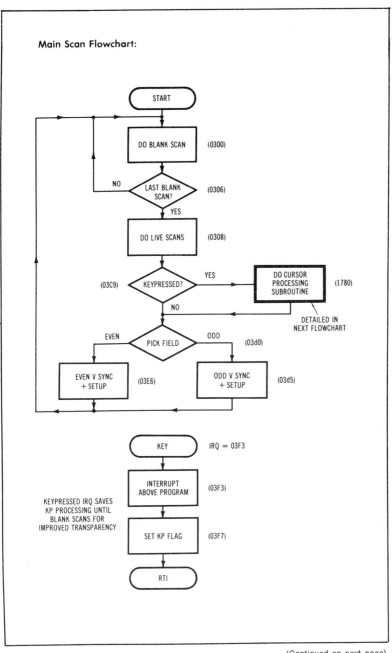

START

DO BLANK SCAN (0300)

LAST BLANK SCAN? (0306)

NO

YES

DO LIVE SCANS (0308)

KEYPRESSED? (03C9)

YES

DO CURSOR PROCESSING SUBROUTINE (1780)

DETAILED IN NEXT FLOWCHART

NO

PICK FIELD (03d0)

EVEN

ODD

EVEN V SYNC + SETUP (03E6)

ODD V SYNC + SETUP (03d5)

KEY   IRQ = 03F3

INTERRUPT ABOVE PROGRAM (03F3)

KEYPRESSED IRQ SAVES KP PROCESSING UNTIL BLANK SCANS FOR IMPROVED TRANSPARENCY

SET KP FLAG (03F7)

RTI

(Continued on next page)

program for the KIM-1 and TVT 6⅝.

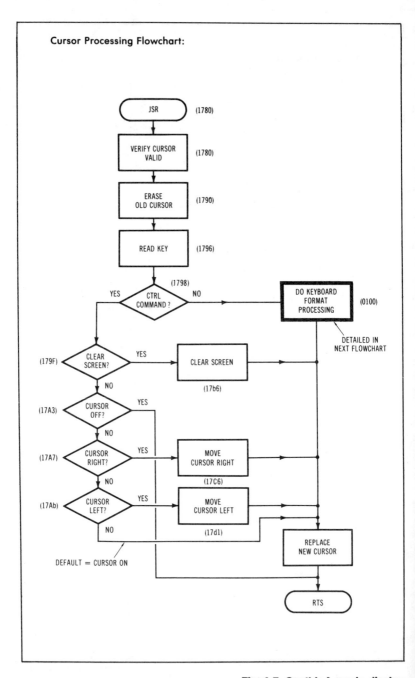

Fig. 4-7. Cont'd. A music display

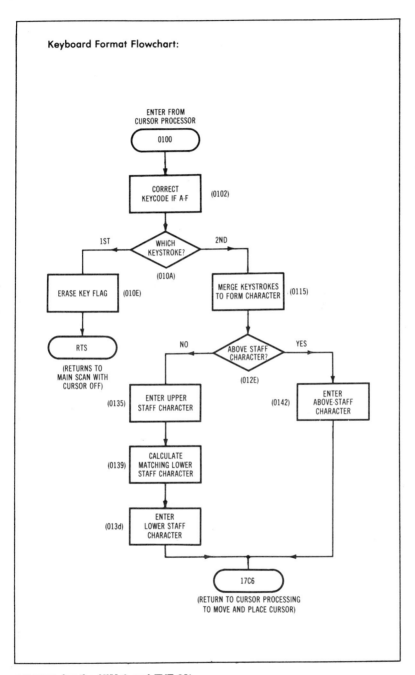

Keyboard Format Flowchart:

ENTER FROM
CURSOR PROCESSOR

0100

CORRECT
KEYCODE IF A-F (0102)

WHICH
KEYSTROKE? (010A)

1ST

2ND

ERASE KEY FLAG (010E)

RTS

(RETURNS TO
MAIN SCAN WITH
CURSOR OFF)

MERGE KEYSTROKES
TO FORM CHARACTER (0115)

ABOVE STAFF
CHARACTER? (012E)

NO

YES

(0135) ENTER UPPER
STAFF CHARACTER

(0142) ENTER
ABOVE-STAFF
CHARACTER

(0139) CALCULATE
MATCHING LOWER
STAFF CHARACTER

(013d) ENTER
LOWER STAFF
CHARACTER

17C6

(RETURN TO CURSOR PROCESSING
TO MOVE AND PLACE CURSOR)

program for the KIM-1 and TVT 6⅝.

terrupted. This is done by connecting the keypressed strobe of the keyboard to the KIM's interrupt line, and pulling the IRQ line briefly low when a new and valid key is down.

After the interrupt, the keyboard is read from the parallel input port and stashed in 00EA. A zero hard-wired on the PA7 automatically flags the "new key" information into 00EA. After some careful timing equalization, the interrupt is then released.

Note that the key closure can happen at any random time with respect to scan timing. This interrupt program catches the key closure "on the fly" and stashes its value until the beginning of the next vertical blanking interval. By waiting until the vertical blanking time, you can gain transparency on your display. With a properly designed cursor software sequence, only a slight bump will be produced at the instant the key is pressed. For this interrupt to work, the IRQ vector must branch to 03F3 on a key closure.

CURSOR PROCESSING—The visual cursor appears as a dotted box on the screen, below the usual staff, and pointing to the location to be modified. A pressed key could be one of a *pair* of key closures that tell us what the next symbol is to be, following the code of Fig. 4-4. The cursor disappears on the first keystroke and reappears on the second, to prevent you from getting one keystroke off. A pressed key could also be a *single* control command that will move the cursor or erase the screen. The cursor processing subroutine finds out whether the key is a control command or part of an entry pair and then acts accordingly.

There are four page zero locations associated with the cursor processing:

00EA—holds the ASCII keyboard command until it is used. The MSB is a flag that is a 0 if the key needs to be acted on.

00Eb—holds the first keystroke in corrected hex form on the lower four bits. The MSB is a flag that is a 0 if the key is the *first* of an entry pair.

00Ed—holds the cursor low needed for *above staff* entry. This value ranges from hex 0A to 3F. The Y index is added to 00Ed for on-staff and below-staff locations.

00EE—holds the cursor high location on page 02.

The cursor processing subroutine is entered when the main scan senses a key-down-but-unprocessed flag (0) in 00EA. The cursor location is then checked to be sure it is valid, and then the keypressed flag is reset. The valid cursor location is needed to prevent plowing another program with a wayward cursor, while the keypressed flag needs to be reset so that the key gets processed only once. After these two steps, the cursor is replaced with a blank in step 1790.

We then read the key in step 1796 and test it to see if it is a control key that will give us cursor motions or an alphanumeric key that is part of a two-stroke symbol entry.

If we do NOT have a control code (ASCII A0 or less), we jump to the upcoming keyboard format processing. If we do have a control code, we test for codes to CLEAR SCREEN (98), CURSOR RIGHT (89), CURSOR LEFT (88), CURSOR OFF (8A), or CURSOR ON (any other CTRL code). Cursor processing goes like this:

* **Clear screen**—The cursor is set to the upper left of the page (17b6) and blank 00 values are stored on the entire page, using the Y index to step the blanks through the page space. The cursor is then set extreme left.

* **Cursor right**—Cursor location flag 00Ed is incremented if the cursor is not already at extreme right. This is also done after symbol entry.

* **Cursor left**—Cursor location flag 00Ed is decremented if the cursor is not already at the extreme left.

* **Cursor off**—The cursor subroutine returns to the scan program immediately without restoring the cursor symbol.

* **Cursor on**—The default option continues the cursor subroutine, replacing the cursor on screen without any motions.

After the cursor motion is complete, the cursor symbol is replaced at its new location, and the subroutine returns to the main scan program.

This particular subroutine has not been fully equalized. You will want to add your own equalization to prevent any screen tearing.

KEYBOARD FORMATTER—You enter the keyboard formatter part of the cursor program by jumping to 0100. This jump takes place if the pressed key was an alphanumeric rather than a control command.

Two keystrokes are needed to enter a hex character, so this portion of the program behaves two different ways, depending on whether it is the *first* or *second* keystroke needed for a symbol. The keyboard formatter program always starts off the same way. It gets the keystroke held in 00EA and converts the ASCII character to its hex equivalent. ASCII numbers 0–9 stay as they are, while ASCII A through F get converted to binary equivalents of decimal 10 through 15.

The keyboard formatter program checks to see if this key was the first or the second needed by checking the most significant flag bit of 00Eb. If the key is the first one, we store its hex-converted value in 00Eb and set the entry pair flag to a 1. This "first-or-second" flag is the most significant bit in 00Eb and tells the software that the *next* key to arrive is the *second* of a needed pair to produce the hex word.

When the second key arrives, it starts the same way, getting corrected to a hex equivalent. The two keys are merged into one hex word in 0127. This is done by shifting the first key value four to the left and then ORing it with the new second key value. The net result is that the two key closures get converted into a hex word equal to the hex code of the wanted symbol.

This hex code is then tested to see if it is an above-staff or an on-staff symbol. If it is an above-staff symbol, it gets entered directly at the cursor location. The keyboard formatter then returns to the cursor subroutine to move the cursor one to the right and then returns to the main scan.

Things are slightly more complicated if the hex code corresponds to an on-staff symbol. First, the hex code gets stored in the proper upper-staff location. Then the equivalent lower-staff symbol needed for the bottom half is calculated by adding hex 80 to the top half symbol code, in step 0139. This new value is then stored on the lower staff. The difference between upper staff and lower staff storage is set by the Y register and a Y indexed storage command. A value of Y=0 puts things above staff. A value of Y=40 puts them on the upper staff. A value of Y=80 goes lower staff, while a value of Y=C0 goes below-staff in the visual cursor position. After the symbol goes on-screen, the cursor is advanced, and control returns to the main scan program.

TEST AND DEBUG

There are several hints for testing your music display software. The most important of these is to *get the scan portion of your display working first*. The software can be *sequentially* debugged by following the notes in Fig. 4-7.

Once things are working, there is a quick and easy way to put a bare staff on the screen. First, clear the screen. Then type a 10. This should give you the left end of the staff. Then *hold* down a "1" and use your keyboard repeat key or auto repeat. This will automatically generate a bare staff across the screen. To finish, wait until the cursor goes *off*. Then type a *single* "3." That should end the staff. Return to the left with the cursor left and repeat commands. You are now ready to write your music.

There are bound to be lots and lots of changes you'll want to make. If you run out of character positions in your EPROM, note that there are lots of redundant character bottoms and tops that can be "patched around" with software. Typical examples are the blank squares, three empty staff lines, and two empty staff lines. These are stored in many EPROM locations, when, in theory, you need only store them once. How many redundant characters are there in the EPROM program as shown?

POLYPHONY

But, how can we show more than one note at a time on the staff? Is there any simple way to let us show polyphonic music as well as the single-notedness we have already picked up?

As usual, the answer is . . . yes, but. . . . Fig. 4-8 shows another sledgehammer. This works but will cost you extra RAM and extra software.

What you do is set up a typical cheap video brute-force high-res graphics system, with its own display memory and a plain old Module "B" graphics output plug-in. Now, put your new EPROM somewhere else in the system, tied in just like any other ROM, EPROM, or RAM to the microcomputer's address and data buses.

To change what goes on the screen, you use your EPROM and some mapping software to reload and change the display memory. You still have nonvolatile characters permanently stashed in your machine. The not-so-obvious new feature you pick up is that you can *superimpose* symbols in the display memory.

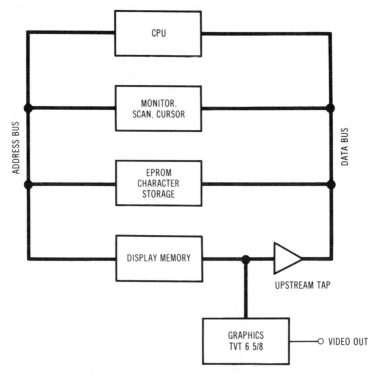

Fig. 4-8. "Sledgehammer" approach to complex graphics displays puts character generator before the display memory to let you add new symbols to ones already existing on the display.

For instance, to put a single note in the display memory, you pick the note you want and decide where you want it to go. Then you use some *map* software to read the EPROM and stash the results in the main display memory. Eight to sixteen reads will be needed for a single transfer. This is easily handled with a software subroutine.

Now, if the screen is empty or a blank staff, you put the new note in, as before. But, if you want to add a second, a third, or any number of new notes to an already existing one, just get the old note out of the *display* memory, *add* or logically OR the stuff to be added from the EPROM *character store*, and then put everything back into the display memory. Your character set will probably be different than the one we've looked at, but it will have a big advantage—far fewer stored symbols are needed to generate a wide variety of composite notes and chords. If you get into animation, this route can also get you smoother results, since the symbols need only move one dot at a time instead of a whole chunk.

All we are really doing here is using an EPROM the way everybody else does, and using a separate hi-res graphics display memory for the final display. This takes much more in the way of RAM and software than you need with cheap video and a custom EPROM character generator, but it offers a powerful way to do elegant and nonvolatile graphics displays of your choosing.

CHAPTER **5**

8080 Cheap Video — Heath H8 Hardware

You'll find things more challenging when you add cheap video to an 8080 or Z80 system, compared to the easy 6500 conversions we have looked at. There are several new hassles involved that can get in your way.

In most cases, these hassles will take extra coding, a few more integrated circuits, and *very* careful attention to your system timing. The bottom line is this: Cheap video should be able to run on most any 8080 or Z80 system, but it will take more effort, more code, and more parts to get comparable results.

Let's see just what is involved. In this chapter, we'll look at the basics of 8080 cheap video operation, ending up with schematics for an adaptor you can put on a Heath H8 computer memory card. We'll also look at some simple hardware mods that ease front-panel interaction and allow serial keyboard entry to your computer. In the next chapter, we'll look at the scan and cursor software involved.

We'll assume your system is bus oriented and that your cheap video system is to be a piggyback add-on to an existing RAM plug-in card. We'll further assume the usual 2-MHz 8080 speed. We will also stick with the earlier address-mapped techniques. The newer scungy video ideas of earlier chapters can very much simplify and improve what we are about to show you. But, first things first.

What we will show you has been tested only on the Heath 50-pin bus. It *looks* like it will also go on an S-100 bus, but we simply haven't tried it.

Our main 8080 hassles are these:

(1) The address bus has garbage on it at times.

(2) The program counter usually can change only once every *two* microseconds. This is only half as fast as we need for a reasonable number of characters or graphics chunks per line.

(3) Clocking and timing signals are totally different.

(4) Literal translation of scan programs will be far too slow.

In general, we will get around (1) by latching and holding both address and upstream tap data lines using suitably spaced timing signals. We can beat (2) by adding a "speed doubling" circuit that creates the *illusion* of a once-per-microsecond program counter advance. This illusion will appear only at the display memory and then only during a TVT scan. Hassle (3) goes away when we solve (2). Finally, we can get scan software that is fast enough by using the powerful register-to-register commands of the 8080 or by going to brute-force (all ROM, nonmodifying) coding.

On to the fine print.

HARDWARE

Suppose we have a normal H8 up and running, executing a string of no operations (NOP) from a plug-in RAM card. What will this timing look like? How can we trick the H8 into using the same sort of timing, with add-ons, to run a TVT 6⅝? Fig. 5-1 gives us some clues.

A NOP takes two microseconds to do—actually slightly less than this on the H8. There are four *CPU States* (Fig. 5-1A) involved, taking around half a microsecond each. The object of these four states is to put the program counter on the address bus, read an addressed memory location, enter it into the CPU, and then act on the command. When the CPU finds out the command is a NOP, it will spend the tail end of the cycle essentially doing nothing.

Our first hassle appears in Fig. 5-1B. We see that the address bus has the right information on it only three quarters of the time. The remaining one quarter of the time, the address bus has invalid information on it. Now, if we address a memory with the wrong address, we, of course, will get the wrong information out of the memory. Worse still, since the memory has its own access time to contend with, the amount of time that *useful* stuff comes out of the memory is even shorter than the time the address bus is valid (Fig. 5-1C). So, the bad news is that both data and address have all kinds of holes in them and don't seem directly useable.

There are some system-level signals that may help us out of this bind. Signal DBIN in Fig. 5-1D determines the time when the CPU *must* have valid data. But, this signal is not available on the system bus and for a very good reason. Anyone who tries to use this signal will be cutting into the CPU's *own* processing time and degrading performance. Instead, two signals are derived for bus use. These signals happen early enough that enables, decoding, settling times, and so on are complete before the CPU needs valid data. These signals are called M1 (Fig. 5-1E), and MEMR (Fig. 5-1F). M1 starts after

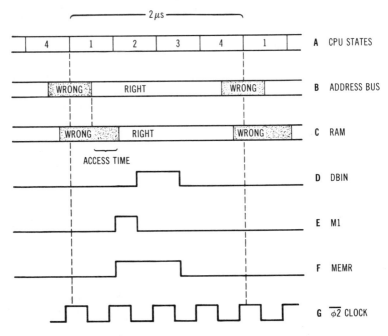

Fig. 5-1. The H8 is a typical 2-MHz system; these are the waveforms involved in reading a NOP command out of RAM.

the address is valid but ends before DBIN. MEMR includes both the M1 and DBIN times. *Unfortunately, both M1 and MEMR start before we are sure that the memory is outputting valid data.* The theory here is that output enables and bus access can be taking place during the *same* time that the memory is still accessing itself, so long as everything ends up stable by the start of DBIN time.

A final waveform we will find useful is the $\overline{\phi 2}$ system clock shown in Fig. 5-1G.

The absolute least thing we can get away with and still get cheap video on an 8080 is latching the upper four address lines. If we don't do this, all the commands out of our TVT instruction decoder PROM, including the row commands and the sync pulses, will have big holes chopped in them.

Fig. 5-2 shows a minimum 8080 to TVT 6⅝ interface. In this circuit, +5 volts, ground, blanking, the upstream tap, and the data bus are connected in the usual way. Address lines A12 through A15 are connected to a latch that catches the valid addresses. This is done on the *leading edge* of the memory read command, MEMR.

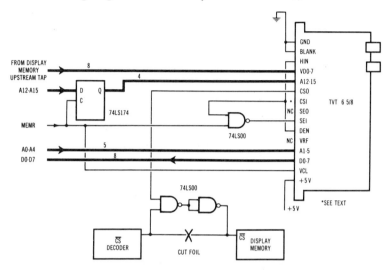

Fig. 5-2. Minimum 8080A-TVT 6⅝ interface is limited to 2-microsecond character or chunk times.

Our chip select output, CSO, is shown going to an AND gate that gives us an external negative logic OR combination of the old display memory chip select and the one needed for TVT scanning. A foil cut is involved here. The chip select input, CSI, is shown permanently enabled. Depending on your decode PROM, this can go to a TVT enable switch, can do nothing, or can be used as an internal chip select combiner, eliminating the external gate.

The TVT is allowed to gain data bus control only during a scan and then only when the computer wants to read it. To do this, we use the computer's memory read command, MEMR, and NAND it with the decode enable, DEN, to get a suitable scan enable input, SEI.

MEMR also goes to the clock input of the TVT 6⅝. But, since our load command in the TVT is derived from the falling edge of VCL, it is the *trailing* edge of MEMR that loads our video shift register. The time difference of 750 nanoseconds or so gives our character generator more than enough time to produce a valid output.

Now, this is a quick and dirty circuit that you may want to try just to get some video out of your 8080 in a hurry. But, there are several problems we still have to attack to get something good enough for normal system use.

One minor hangup is that you may only have complements of your data bus or address bus available. We'll soon see how to change the coding in your Scan and Decode PROMs to get around this. The coding, of course, has to be changed anyway, since the 8080 gets all bent out of shape when it receives 6502 commands. Inverters or inverting gates can also be used to invert bus, clock, data, or control lines as needed. If you go the scungy video route via a port, you may be able to eliminate any need for high addresses.

Our big hassle is that the character or chunk times will be *two* microseconds each, rather than just one. This means that, so far, even a 32 character line won't run at normal horizontal scan frequencies. Beating this particular hassle soundly about the head and ears is the key to practical cheap video on the 8080.

But how?

SPEED DOUBLING VIA A9 SWITCHING

We want to get our chunk and character times down to a decent one microsecond. We can either (1) speed up the microprocessor, or else (2) do something else that creates the *illusion* of a microprocessor speedup at the display memory and in the adaptor circuits.

Speedup may be easy for you if you have a Z80, provided your display memory is also fast enough to not use the READY command. If you do run faster, you probably would like to latch the upstream tap data to make sure you have enough processing time for your character generator. While a simple speedup will work in some systems, there is another way.

The other way is called *A9 switching*.

The object of A9 switching is to create the *illusion* of a once per microsecond address advance at the display memory. Fig. 5-3 gives details on how this works. We break our most significant display space address line and connect it to a carefully timed 500-kHz square wave during a scan. For a 16 × 64 or a 12 × 80 alphanumeric display, this will be address line A9.

Now, a 500-kHz square wave is low for one microsecond and high for another one. While all the regular addresses *below* A9 are changing at their usual *two* microsecond rate, A9 is busy addressing one character or chunk location on the first microsecond and another location on the second. Thus, we get characters or chunks out of our display memory at a one per microsecond clip.

But why on earth use A9? Wouldn't it be simpler to use A0 instead? If we do this, we would have to add an address multiplexer to all inputs of this display memory—a 10-pole, double-throw switch or its three-state equivalent. This is obviously something we want to avoid if we are piggy-backing video onto an existing memory card. All A9 switching takes is a single foil cut and some add-on wires to the memory card.

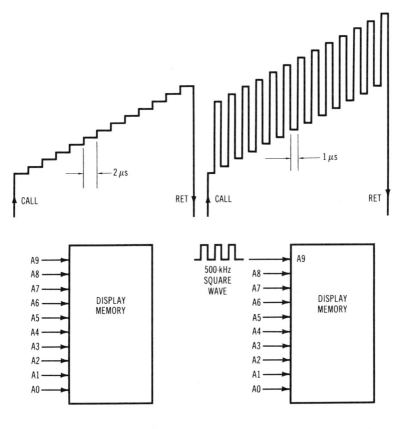

DURING A SCAN, ADDRESSES ADVANCE ONLY ONCE EVERY TWO MICROSECONDS, TOO SLOW TO OUTPUT CHARACTERS.

DURING A SCAN, 500-kHz CLOCK ON A9 LINE PRODUCES NEW ADDRESS EACH MICROSECOND; CHARACTERS OUTPUT AT PROPER RATE.

(A) Normal 8080 operation.   (B) A9 switched 8080 operation.

Fig. 5-3. How to use A9 switching for speedup.

There is a catch. It is a yeahbut rather than a gotcha. *The characters and chunks are no longer in the display memory in sequential order if you use A9 switching.* So, your cursor or controlling loader software has to have a few words added to complement A9 each successive location.

For instance, say your display memory starts at 000 000. The next character or chunk will be at 002 000. Your characters will follow in this order:

1st	character	000 000
2nd	character	002 000
3rd	character	000 001
4th	character	002 001
5th	character	000 002
6th	character	002 002

.   .

.   .

.   .

1022nd	character	003 376
1023rd	character	001 377
1024th	character	003 377

Now, this sounds awful. But it works. And it is a rather simple way to double the apparent memory access speed of an 8080 so that we can get information out of RAM once per microsecond under block access. And all it takes is some extra hardware between the computer and the TVT, a few software words, and one extra foil cut on the memory.

The hardware involved is shown in Fig. 5-4. The timing details are in Fig. 5-5.

Two new D flip-flops are added to our interface. The first delays and expands the MEMR signal to give us a controlled-phase 500-kHz square wave we can use for the speed doubling A9 address switching. The second divides the system clock by two and is used to latch the video data and to provide a TVT clock.

Waveforms A, B, C, and D are as before. Waveform E is a $\phi2$ clock, which has to be an inverted replica of the Heath bus $\phi2$ clock signal. Waveform F shows the 500-kHz square wave that results when we clock MEMR. Since the clocking is delayed from the MEMR leading edge, the flip-flop's output is wider than MEMR and turns out almost a microsecond long. This results in a square wave that is low for one microsecond and high for the next, locked to (but following) MEMR.

This particular flip-flop is allowed to run only *during* a scan. It is held high by DEN otherwise. The uppermost two gates combine the old A9 information with the speed-doubling new A9 signal, acting as a single-pole, double-throw selector switch. During computer times, the display memory A9 line is connected to the computer. During scan microinstruction times, the display memory A9 line is connected so that it is low for one microsecond and high for the next.

Waveform G shows the one-megahertz clock we get by dividing down $\phi 2$. This clock is used to sample and latch the display memory

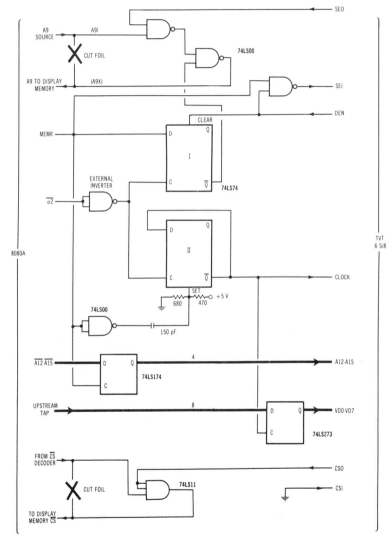

Fig. 5-4. Speed-doubling 8080A-TVT 6⅝ interface gives 1-microsecond character or chunk times.

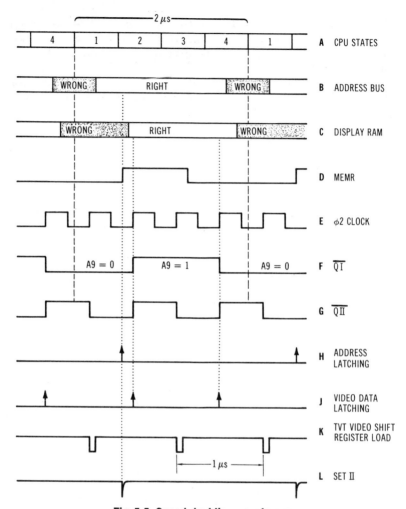

Fig. 5-5. Speed-doubling waveforms.

output immediately after the data is valid, and then latch again one microsecond later, well after the A9 change has been accepted. The first sample gives us an A9 = 0 data value, while the second handles the A9 = 1 case. The TVT's video shift register is clocked on the falling edge of this one-megahertz clock. Since there is a half microsecond delay between the leading and trailing clock edges, enough time is available for the character generator or the data-to-video converter to accept the latched video data and process it.

Our A9 generating flip-flop automatically initializes itself on MEMR since it is simply delaying this signal. But the clock dividing flip-flop could be in either state at the *beginning* of a scan microinstruction. Unless we somehow initialize this flip-flop to the right state, we'll get garbage out of the display memory caused by sampling at the wrong times.

We initialize this clock-dividing flip-flop by inverting MEMR and using the leading edge to SET the divide flip-flop to the desired state. This initialization is very important, since the usual CALL in-

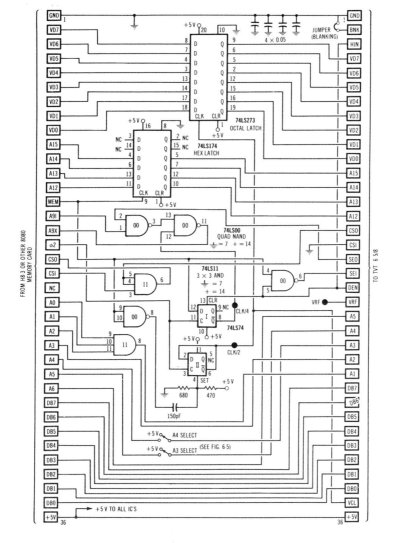

Fig. 5-6. Schematic of 8080/cheap-video adaptor.

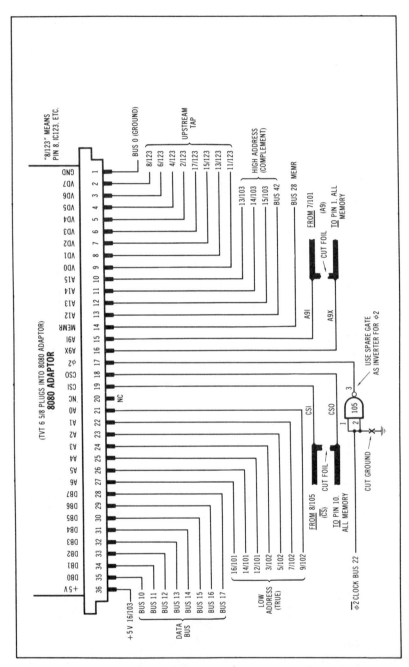

Fig. 5-7. Pictorial of 8080 adaptor interface to Heath H8-3 memory card.

struction preceding the scan microinstruction has an odd number of clock cycles in it.

TVT scan enabling and the display memory chip selecting are done the same way we did in the slower interface of Fig. 5-2. We enable the TVT Scan Enable Input (SEI) only during MEMR time to give us data for a scan microinstruction only when it is called for and only when the computer will allow data bus access. The display memory chip select is a negative logic OR of the computer's chip select and the CSO that the TVT provides.

Our speed-doubling interface takes two foil cuts on the memory board, one on the A9 address line and one on the chip select line. All other connections are add-ons derived from signals available on a typical plug-in memory card. Five low-cost integrated circuits are involved.

A more detailed schematic of an H8 to TVT 6⅝ interface is shown in Fig. 5-6. This circuit can be built up any way you like. One possibility is as a small plug-in card that goes between your H8 and the TVT 6⅝. The TVT card plugs into the 8080 adaptor, and then the 8080 adaptor plugs into a new connector that piggybacks onto the H8-3 static RAM card. The video circuits can easily be mounted on the back of the existing RAM card.

Fig. 5-7 shows a pictorial of the connections to your H8-3 RAM card, while Fig. 5-8 gives details on how and where to make the

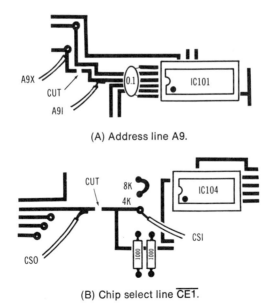

(A) Address line A9.

(B) Chip select line $\overline{CE1}$.

Fig. 5-8. Two foil cuts needed on the H8-3 memory card.

two foil cuts involved on the address A9 and memory Chip Select ($\overline{CS}$) lines.

Interconnection and mounting details will vary if you use one of the newer or denser RAM cards, or if you work with another 8080, 8085, or Z80 system.

FRONT-PANEL INTERACTION

The H8 front panel works by interrupting a running program once very two milliseconds. If we try to run scan software and the front panel at the same time, the display will be badly torn up. So, we can either turn the front panel off during display times or else combine the front panel and the video scan into a single program. Just turning the front panel off is far simpler and usually all you will need.

The H8 front-panel monitor does have a "turn the display off" software word. But this won't help us. While this command shortens the interrupt and keeps it from lighting the display, the interrupt still exists.

One hardware solution is shown in Fig. 5-9. A new switch added to the front panel prevents timer-generated level 10 interrupts from happening. This, in turn, keeps the panel display off and the video display in one piece. This switch will be very handy during your initial test and debugging of video displays. You should turn *off* the front panel only after you have a video display, and turn it back *on* before returning to other uses. The RST/0 command does bypass this switch so that you can reset under any conditions.

This switch will most likely *not* be needed when your properly designed and debugged scan software is up and running. You probably can eliminate it from the final use circuitry.

The obvious question is how to use software instead. We have a good old DI or "disable interrupts" command in the 8080 instruction set. Can't we simply use this?

Unfortunately, there is one very noisy gotcha that may keep you from doing this—unless you are careful.

If you try an immediate DI command in an H8 program, the speaker will latch on and *stay* on. That little beep you get when you hit the GO key—or any other key—needs *two* more interrupts *after* your program starts. No interrupts, no stopping. The two interrupts time out a four-millisecond tick for the horn circuit.

So, a rule:

The H8 front-panel monitor needs a few milliseconds *after* it is exited before you can disable any interrupts. If you disable an interrupt too soon, you will lock the speaker on.

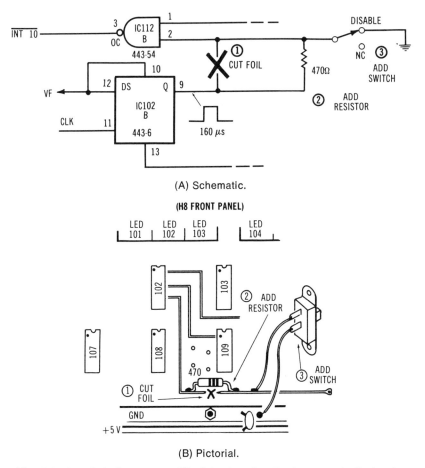

(A) Schematic.

(H8 FRONT PANEL)

(B) Pictorial.

Fig. 5-9. A switch for temporarily defeating the H8 front-panel display is useful for TVT debug and checkout.

You can use the DI command to turn off the front panel. But you must delay at least five milliseconds *after* your program starts, or the speaker won't quit. Thus, one properly placed software word is all you need to get full front-panel and video-display compatibility.

A KEYBOARD SERIAL ADAPTOR

If you have an H8-2 parallel interface card, it should be fairly easy to attach most any old ASCII keyboard and encoder. You can do

141

this in much the same way we did on the parallel KIM inputs in *The Cheap Video Cookbook*.

But, the H8-2 card is an expensive option, and you might not already have one on hand. More likely, you will be using the H8-5 serial interface card instead, since you need this one for the usual cassette and remote terminal uses.

Most ASCII keyboards and encoders provide only a parallel (all the bits at once) output. To enter a serial port, we have to convert this parallel word into a serial (one bit at a time) sequence. A simple keyboard serial adaptor is shown in Fig. 5-10.

The circuit can use the transmitter half of most any old UART. UART stands for *Universal Asynchronous Receiver Transmitter*. We first looked at these way back in Chapter 7 of the *TV Typewriter Cookbook*. You'll find this circuit easiest and cheapest when you use a modern, single-supply CMOS chip such as an Intersil IM6402 or IM6403.

The keyboard serial adaptor works by borrowing power from the H8-5 serial interface and feeding +5 volts and optionally −12 volts to your existing keyboard. The parallel outputs and a normally high *keypressed* strobe are routed to the inputs on the transmitter side of the UART in the adaptor. The same UART borrows a 16× baud clock from the H8-3.

As many as five leads will be needed between your adaptor and the H8-5. One is ground, one or two are for power, one is for the 16× baud rate clock *from* computer *to* adaptor, and the final lead is the serial output that comes *from* adaptor *to* computer.

Fig. 5-11 shows how to connect your adaptor to your H8-5, both pictorially and schematically. You can either hard-wire connections or add a new connector of your own.

On your H8-5 board, integrated circuit IC122 is removed and replaced with two jumpers inserted in the socket as shown. The pin 11 to pin 13 jumper gives you direct access to the serial input in the computer's circuitry. The pin 6 to pin 7 jumper lets you use the keyboard in a *polled* mode. This polled operation gives you a transparent scan program and frees the interrupts for other uses.

The H8 has to be software programmed to use your new adaptor. A simple test sequence that will enter the last pressed key into the accumulator and display it for you is shown in Fig. 5-12.

The H8-5 is first initialized with a *mode* instruction. You can use 312 and output it to port 373. This picks two stop bits, ignores parity, uses a seven-bit word, and runs with a 16× clock. Next, you continue to initialize the H8-5 by giving a *command* instruction to the same port. This time, use 004 and once again output it to port 373. This command instruction will enable only the receiver in the H8-5 interface.

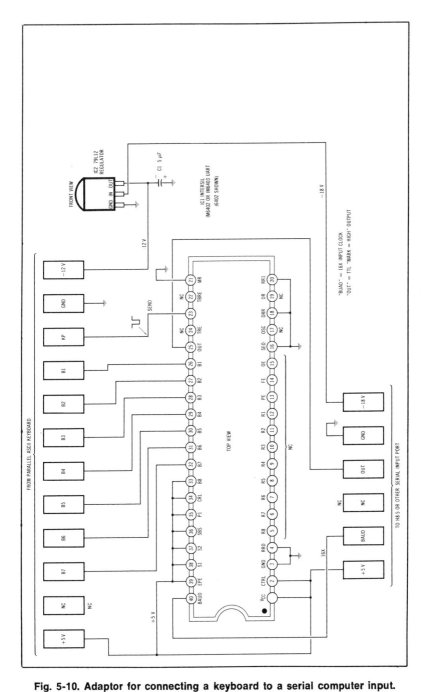

Fig. 5-10. Adaptor for connecting a keyboard to a serial computer input.

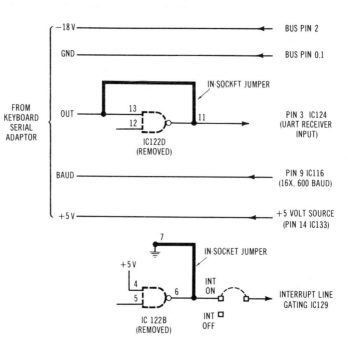

(A) Schematic.

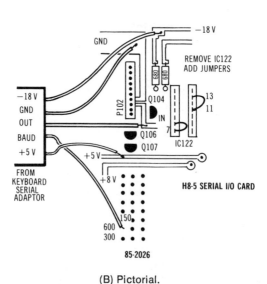

(B) Pictorial.

Fig. 5-11. Connecting keyboard serial adaptor to an H8-5 interface.

After the mode instruction and the command instruction are routed to the interface, you are free to read characters. You do this by inputting from port 372. The final loop in the test program does this continuously.

As you press a key, its ASCII value will appear in the left three digits of the "AF" Register display. For instance, a lower case "b" will read as 142, while an upper case "B" will read as 102.

```
μP—8080A              Start—JMP 040  100      Program Space
System—H8 + H8-5      End—RST/0                040  100 to 040  113
                                                    (13 words)

START ——040  100     MVIA 076  312      Initialize mode instruction
        040  102     OUT  323  373          continued
        040  104     MVIA 076  004      Initialize command instruction
        040  106     OUT  323  373          continued

      ┌—040  110     IN   333  372      Read keyboard
      └—040  112     JMP  303  (110)(040)  Loop
```

Notes:

This test program displays a pressed key received via the Keyboard Serial Adaptor. To run the program, use:

RST/0—REG—PC—ALTER—0—4—0—
1—0—0—ALTER—REG—AF—GO.

ASCII characters should appear as the three leftmost digits on the display. For instance, "A" = 101, "a" = 141, "6" = 066, and "CR" = 015.

( ) Denotes an absolute address that is relocation sensitive.

Fig. 5-12. Keyboard serial adaptor test program.

There are a few gotchas in this simple test program, so you'll want to improve it for actual use as part of a cursor. Note that this simple program continuously *re-reads* characters over and over again instead of just once per character.

To beat this, there is a "character ready" (R × RDY) flag available that is set when the character first arrives and is reset as soon as the computer uses the character for the first time.

To use a character only once, input from port 373, AND what you get with 002, and test the result. A nonzero result means you have a new character ready to enter. A zero result says you have already used the character on hand and should ignore it.

The UART doing the transmitting (in the adaptor) and the one doing the receiving (in the H8-5) must agree on the baud rate and the baud clock factor. Usually, the H8-5 will be set on 600 baud and 16× clocks with internal jumpers. If not, or if you are on a different system, be sure that the transmitting UART and the receiving UART are on speaking terms with each other.

Note that your initialization of the *mode* and *command* words should be done only once after reset and before any input/output activity. If you don't initialize, you'll get no characters at all, and if you continuously reinitialize, characters will get dumped before you can use them.

Your keyboard serial adaptor is very flexible. For instance, go over the data sheets, and you'll find a whole UART receiver unused on the low number pins. The −12 volt supply is an option. You can eliminate it if you already have −12 volts on hand or use a keyboard that doesn't need it. You can also use the old style UARTs that need −12 volts by removing the connections on pin 2 and jumpering to −12 volts.

Should you use the IM6403, you can eliminate the 16× baud rate line by connecting a 3.58 MHz color tv crystal between pins 17 and 40 while grounding pin 3. This will output characters for you at 110 baud. Your computer's serial input will also have to be jumpered or programmed to use this new data rate.

As shown, the keyboard serial adaptor is programmed to provide a permanent one in the transmitted ASCII bit number 8, is continuously enabled, has no parity, uses two stop bits, and has an eight-bit word length. You can change any or all of this by reprogramming the connections on pins 33 through 39 of the UART. Our circuit assumes the keyboard outputs positive logic and uses a narrow goes-to-ground-from-positive-high strobe that is low only when data is valid. The output is a simple TTL logic level. There is no need to convert to RS232 or Teletype current loops for a short interface connection.

Your Turn:

Show how to use your keyboard serial adaptor with only *two* wires between computer and keyboard, *including all power supply connections.* (HINT: Use the IM6403 with a crystal and a CMOS encoded keyboard. Change the current when you want to send a zero, and sense this current at the computer end.)

Or, if you really want to get sneaky, you could try to figure out a way to have *zero* connections between your keyboard and your computer. One way you might do this would be to use ultrasonic or infrared transducers.

CHAPTER **6**

8080 Cheap Video —
Heath H8 Software

We now have some workable hardware for 8080 cheap video operation. Let's turn to the software we will need to get our scan programs and cursor controllers.

In this chapter, we'll stick to the older cheap video techniques of address mapping and subroutine scanning. We will also use an obvious but inefficient brute-force program method to give us nonvolatile scan programs that do not self-modify. Once you have scan programs that work, it's a simple matter to go on to the newer scungy video ideas, to minimize address space use, to improve transparency, and to write short and efficient self-modifying programs. The strong input/output commands in the 8030A, along with its 16-bit-wide register pairs, offer all sorts of new software opportunities for short and efficient cheap video software.

If we use the old address mapping of *The Cheap Video Cookbook*, a typical computer memory map is shown in Fig. 6-1. A block of addresses from 6K to 60K is reserved for TVT use when the TVT is enabled. On the H8, this leaves the bottom 8K for the PAM monitor and operating system, and 16K for enough RAM for both a display memory and Extended BASIC. The uppermost 4K of addresses are also available as needed.

Later on, we can dramatically minimize the address space needs by using the new scungy video ideas of Chapters 1 and 2.

A quick look at the H8-3 memory board shows that only some of the address and data lines are available in their true form. Most of them are inverted. The data out buffer on this memory card must be disabled for the upstream tap needed by cheap video. This means that the output of our Scan Microinstruction PROM (if we use one) has to drive the system data bus directly and thus must output inverted (negative logic) data. We also see that address lines A13, A14, and A15 aren't available except as complements. The simplest way out of this situation is to code our *Decode* PROM to respond directly to complemented addresses.

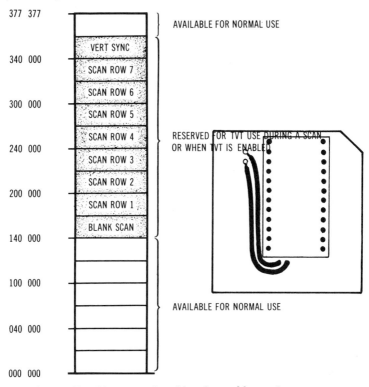

377 377   AVAILABLE FOR NORMAL USE

VERT SYNC

340 000

SCAN ROW 7

SCAN ROW 6

300 000

SCAN ROW 5

SCAN ROW 4   RESERVED FOR TVT USE DURING A SCAN

240 000   OR WHEN TVT IS ENABLED

SCAN ROW 3

SCAN ROW 2

200 000

SCAN ROW 1

BLANK SCAN

140 000

100 000   AVAILABLE FOR NORMAL USE

040 000

000 000

Fig. 6-1. H8 address map for older cheap video system.

Fig. 6-2 shows the H8 Decode PROM truth table, 658-HD8. We input lines $\overline{A12}$, $\overline{A13}$, $\overline{A14}$, and $\overline{A15}$, along with a TVT enable using the old CSI line. This PROM outputs code to the row commands of the character generator, or else routes blanking and selection commands to a graphics data-to-video converter. The Decode PROM also outputs system controlling signals DEN, SEO, CSO, and the vertical sync VRF pulses.

Since we are using complemented address inputs, this PROM runs "backwards" from the earlier PROMs. The net result of a "frontwards" PROM with true address inputs or a "backwards" PROM with inverted address inputs is the same.

INPUTS				OUTPUTS							
	WORD #	WHAT DOES THIS WORD DO?	HEX OP-CODE	Q8 CS OUT	Q7 SCAN ENABLE	Q6 DECODE ENABLE	Q5 VERTICAL SYNC	Q4 (SPARE)	Q3 CG LINE 4	Q2 CG LINE 2	Q1 CG LINE 1
TVT ENABLED	0	NORMAL	C0	1	1	0	0	0	0	0	0
	1	VERTICAL SYNC	d0	1	1	0	1	0	0	0	0
	2	LINE 7 SCAN	27	0	0	1	0	0	1	1	1
	3	LINE 6 SCAN	26	0	0	1	0	0	1	1	0
	4	LINE 5 SCAN	25	0	0	1	0	0	1	0	1
	5	LINE 4 SCAN	24	0	0	1	0	0	1	0	0
	6	LINE 3 SCAN	23	0	0	1	0	0	0	1	1
	7	LINE 2 SCAN	22	0	0	1	0	0	0	1	0
	8	LINE 1 SCAN	21	0	0	1	0	0	0	0	1
	9	BLANK SCAN	20	0	0	1	0	0	0	0	0
	10	NORMAL	C0	1	1	0	0	0	0	0	0
	11	NORMAL	C0	1	1	0	0	0	0	0	0
	12	NORMAL	C0	1	1	0	0	0	0	0	0
	13	NORMAL	C0	1	1	0	0	0	0	0	0
	14	NORMAL	C0	1	1	0	0	0	0	0	0
	15	NORMAL	C0	1	1	0	0	0	0	0	0
TVT DISABLED	16	NORMAL	C0	1	1	0	0	0	0	0	0
	17	NORMAL	C0	1	1	0	0	0	0	0	0
	18	NORMAL	C0	1	1	0	0	0	0	0	0
	19	NORMAL	C0	1	1	0	0	0	0	0	0
	20	NORMAL	C0	1	1	0	0	0	0	0	0
	21	NORMAL	C0	1	1	0	0	0	0	0	0
	22	NORMAL	C0	1	1	0	0	0	0	0	0
	23	NORMAL	C0	1	1	0	0	0	0	0	0
	24	NORMAL	C0	1	1	0	0	0	0	0	0
	25	NORMAL	C0	1	1	0	0	0	0	0	0
	26	NORMAL	C0	1	1	0	0	0	0	0	0
	27	NORMAL	C0	1	1	0	0	0	0	0	0
	28	NORMAL	C0	1	1	0	0	0	0	0	0
	29	NORMAL	C0	1	1	0	0	0	0	0	0
	30	NORMAL	C0	1	1	0	0	0	0	0	0
	31	NORMAL	C0	1	1	0	0	0	0	0	0

658-HD8
PROM NUMBER

□ = "0"
■ = "1"
(POSITIVE LOGIC)

Use for TVT 6 5/8 on an 8080 system with inverted $\overline{A12}$, $\overline{A13}$, $\overline{A14}$, $\overline{A15}$ lines.

CG line 2 is used as graphics blanking output.

CG line 4 is used as graphics upper-lower chunk select output.

Fig. 6-2. Truth table for optional 8080 Decode PROM having inverted address inputs (used on Heath H8).

Holding the CSI line positive disables the TVT and frees most all addresses for other uses. Grounding CSI enables the TVT scanning and reserves the needed address blocks for TVT use. This particular PROM coding needs an external AND gate for chip selection and combination.

There are two types of *Scan* PROM coding we might like to use, depending on whether we are using "binary" line lengths or are repacking "nonbinary" line lengths for maximum memory efficiency. Fig. 6-3 shows a Scan PROM coding intended for 64 character lines, but useable for 32 character lines, most graphics, and other lengths *without* memory repacking. This is numbered 658-HS64. We use a NOP to advance the program counter in the computer and a RET coding to return from the called scan microinstruction. Since we are outputting complemented data, these outputs are inverted. On the H8, address lines A0 through A6 are available in true form, so we do not have to complement the address inputs. Thus, our scan PROMs run "frontwards" but output complemented code.

We can use the 658-HS80 Scan PROM truth table of Fig. 6-4 for memory repacked scans of 80 characters per line, three lines per page. Once again, this PROM coding is driven by true addresses and outputs complementary data directly to the H8 $\overline{\text{data}}$ bus.

Our address lines are connected differently on an 8080 system than on a 6502. Remember that we used every *second* address change on the 6502 to advance our Scan PROM *one* count. On an 8080 we use *every* address change to advance the Scan PROM *one* count, but we use A9 switching to get two characters out of memory per one Scan PROM count advance. Either way, the Scan PROM responds to an input address change once every *two* microseconds, and everything comes out even.

This means that, in general on an 8080 system, the Scan PROM's inputs are usually connected to one address line *less* than usual for a 6502 system. Fig. 6-5 shows our address line management for an 8080 adaptor. It also shows how two new switches can be added along with a gate to let you use either a 658-HS64 or a 658-HS80 Scan PROM on an 8080 system without needing any rewiring. Several examples will show how this address management works:

* For 32 character lines using speed doubling, use PROM 658-HS64 and set your switches as follows: A4 = "+," A5 = "+," and "32."
* For 64 character lines using speed doubling, use PROM 658-HS64 and set your switches to A4 = "A4," A5 = "+," and "32."
* For 80 character lines using speed doubling and memory repacking, use PROM 658-HS80 and set your switches to A4 = "A4," A5 = "A5," and "64."

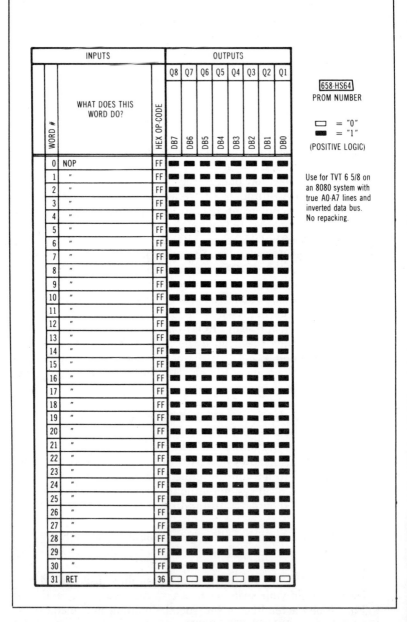

	INPUTS			OUTPUTS								
				Q8	Q7	Q6	Q5	Q4	Q3	Q2	Q1	
WORD #	WHAT DOES THIS WORD DO?	HEX OP-CODE		DB7	DB6	DB5	DB4	DB3	DB2	DB1	DB0	
0	NOP	FF										
1	"	FF										
2	"	FF										
3	"	FF										
4	"	FF										
5	"	FF										
6	"	FF										
7	"	FF										
8	"	FF										
9	"	FF										
10	"	FF										
11	"	FF										
12	"	FF										
13	"	FF										
14	"	FF										
15	"	FF										
16	"	FF										
17	"	FF										
18	"	FF										
19	"	FF										
20	"	FF										
21	"	FF										
22	"	FF										
23	"	FF										
24	"	FF										
25	"	FF										
26	"	FF										
27	"	FF										
28	"	FF										
29	"	FF										
30	"	FF										
31	RET	36										

658-HS64
PROM NUMBER

▭ = "0"
▬ = "1"
(POSITIVE LOGIC)

Use for TVT 6 5/8 on an 8080 system with true A0-A7 lines and inverted data bus. No repacking.

Fig. 6-3. Truth table for optional 8080 Scan PROM having no repacking, true address inputs, and inverted data outputs.

INPUTS			OUTPUTS							
			Q8	Q7	Q6	Q5	Q4	Q3	Q2	Q1
WORD #	WHAT DOES THIS WORD DO?	HEX OP-CODE	DB7	DB6	DB5	DB4	DB3	DB2	DB1	DB0
0	NOP	FF	■	■	■	■	■	■	■	■
1	"	FF	■	■	■	■	■	■	■	■
2	"	FF	■	■	■	■	■	■	■	■
3	"	FF	■	■	■	■	■	■	■	■
4	"	FF	■	■	■	■	■	■	■	■
5	"	FF	■	■	■	■	■	■	■	■
6	"	FF	■	■	■	■	■	■	■	■
7	"	FF	■	■	■	■	■	■	■	■
8	"	FF	■	■	■	■	■	■	■	■
9	"	FF	■	■	■	■	■	■	■	■
10	"	FF	■	■	■	■	■	■	■	■
11	RET	36	□	□	■	■	□	■	■	□
12	NOP	FF	■	■	■	■	■	■	■	■
13	"	FF	■	■	■	■	■	■	■	■
14	"	FF	■	■	■	■	■	■	■	■
15	"	FF	■	■	■	■	■	■	■	■
16	"	FF	■	■	■	■	■	■	■	■
17	"	FF	■	■	■	■	■	■	■	■
18	"	FF	■	■	■	■	■	■	■	■
19	"	FF	■	■	■	■	■	■	■	■
20	"	FF	■	■	■	■	■	■	■	■
21	RET	36	□	□	■	■	□	■	■	□
22	NOP	FF	■	■	■	■	■	■	■	■
23	"	FF	■	■	■	■	■	■	■	■
24	"	FF	■	■	■	■	■	■	■	■
25	"	FF	■	■	■	■	■	■	■	■
26	"	FF	■	■	■	■	■	■	■	■
27	"	FF	■	■	■	■	■	■	■	■
28	"	FF	■	■	■	■	■	■	■	■
29	"	FF	■	■	■	■	■	■	■	■
30	"	FF	■	■	■	■	■	■	■	■
31	RET	36	□	□	■	■	□	■	■	□

658-HS80
PROM NUMBER

□ = "0"
■ = "1"
(POSITIVE LOGIC)

Use only for 80 character repacked lines on an 8080 system with true A0-A7 lines and inverted data bus.

Fig. 6-4. Truth table for optional 80-character 8080 Scan PROM. (True address inputs; inverted data outputs.)

In our first example, the upper half of a Scan PROM is cycled through in 16 counts lasting 32 microseconds. In the second example, the entire Scan PROM is cycled through in 32 counts lasting 64 microseconds. In the final example, if we wanted to, the entire Scan PROM could be scanned in 32 counts lasting 256 microseconds. But with memory repacking and A9 switching, we only use slightly under

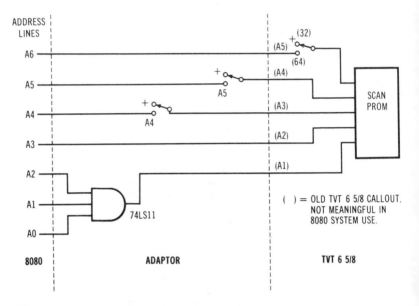

Fig. 6-5. The Scan PROM address inputs on the TVT 6⅝ have to be redefined for 8080 use. The gate and switches let you run ordinary or repacked memory PROMs without wiring changes.

a third of the 80 line Scan PROM *per scan,* ending up with 10 counts per scan lasting 80 microseconds.

Your Turn:

> Show the Scan PROM truth table and switch settings for an H8 scan of 40 repacked characters per line.

Note that the Decode PROM can be eliminated by going the scungy video route of using a port to set the character generator row and sync lines. The Scan PROM can also be eliminated by selecting one of the alternate routes to a scungy video display map outlined in Fig. 1-6.

Let's stay with the old way for our software examples.

TEST SOFTWARE

Two useful test routines are shown in Fig. 6-6. Fig. 6-6A checks Scan PROM access and operation. If this test fails, you are either incorrectly picking up scan microinstructions or are missing them entirely. Erratic switching between 311 (return) and 000 (no operation) means you have speed-doubling problems. All 000's means you are never activating the Scan PROM, while all 311's means you are

---

A. To Verify That the Scan Microinstruction Is Alive and Well

    Read

              300 376   for   000   (NOP)
              300 377   for   311   (RET)
              301 000   for   000   (NOP)

Either the HS64 or the HS80 Scan PROM may be used.
The address switches may be in any position.

B. To Pass Control to and From the Scan Microinstruction at a TV Horizontal Rate

              | For Scan PROM HS64 |

Set switches to "32," A5 = "+," and A4 = "A4."

START→┌─040 100   CALL 315 010 320   Scan seventh dot row
     └─040 103   JMP   303 100 040   Repeat

              | For Scan PROM HS80 |

Set switches to "64," A5 = "A5," A4 = "A4."

START→┌─040 100   CALL 315 030 320   Scan seventh dot row
     └─040 103   JMP   303 100 040   Repeat

This will display continuous vertical stripes that correspond to the seventh dot row of a random character load. The front panel should be switch disabled during viewing times.

H8 scan time is 63 microseconds for a horizontal scan frequency of 15.898 kHz. There is no vertical sync in this test program.

Fig. 6-6. Two test routines useful in 8080/TVT debugging.

permanently trying to return from a scan microinstruction call. This particular test works with either HS64 or HS80 Scan PROMs and can have the address switches in any position.

```
Your Turn:


                            Why?
```

Don't ever try going beyond this test if the test fails. If you cannot read the proper return from a scan microinstruction, no way will it execute, and anything else you add in the way of software or time or effort will only compound the hassle.

The test sequence in Fig. 6-6B lets you transfer control of the H8 from computer to TVT scanning and back again. Note that the test coding differs for each Scan PROM and that each Scan PROM has to have the address switches set as shown.

The scanning process is adjusted to output a tv horizontal scan at normal scan frequencies. In a completely working system with a disabled front panel, you'll get a continuous series of vertical stripes. This corresponds to the seventh dot row of a random character load. A wildly wrong horizontal scan frequency usually means the wrong switch settings or the wrong Scan PROM. Vertical stripes that have teeth in them may be caused by erratic data latching or improper speed-doubling operation.

While these two tests appear trivially simple, don't overlook them as major debug aids. If these two won't go, no other software will run, either.

SELF-MODIFYING VERSUS BRUTE-FORCE SCANS

The obvious next thing to do is take the old 6502 scan software programs and literally translate them, replacing a CALL for a JSR and so on. But we really get into trouble in a hurry if we try this. First off, some commands will be longer or shorter than their 6502 counterparts, messing up the critical horizontal-edge to horizontal-edge timing. But, worse yet, the execution time of an 8080 working with literally translated 6502 commands is p-i-t-i-f-u-l-l-y s-l-o-w.

So slow that the critical timing loop may take over 30 microseconds, compared to the 21 used in the 6502. Which makes the long horizontal lines so long we don't want to even think about using them.

One solution is to make the 8080 into an 8080 rather than an imitation 6502. You can do this using the fast register-to-register transfer commands and get your loop times down only slightly longer than those in the 6502 programs.

But is this really what we want in an 8080 system? Remember that on a bare-bones KIM-1 our back was to the wall in finding room for a scan program. We *had* to get by with the absolute minimum length scan programs—in order to get any video at all. One apparent result of this restriction was that our early scan code was *self-modifying*. This meant that the scan program computed its next set of memory locations rather than looking them up. Which, in turn, meant that these early scan programs *had* to be in RAM during final operation, at least on a KIM.

Usually our 8080 systems have enough RAM and PROM available that we needn't worry too much about minimizing code. So, why not use *brute-force* coding that calls each scan address as it is needed? We can store the whole scan program in ROM or PROM this way and never have to load it again. Or worry about it bombing when something bad happens in RAM.

Brute-force coding will also be much faster. It will be much easier to write, modify, and debug. But, as usual, there is a price. Brute-force coding can be much longer than self-modifying coding. On a one-line display, this turns out to be a no-hassle 43 words versus the 30 words we needed on a KIM with self-modifying code. But, on a long and involved program such as a 24 × 80 double stuffed scan, it could take 600 or more words of code to get us by. Still, that's only a little over a quarter of a 2716 EPROM and no real big deal these days.

Let's use this somewhat primitive brute-force approach to generate a simple one-line display and then apply it to a 12 × 80 scan program.

1 × 56 SCAN PROGRAM

Fig. 6-7 shows a brute-force scan program for a 1-line, 56 character, no-interlace 8080/TVT 6⅝ display. Each successive dot row is called by a scan subroutine as it is needed. We start in 040 100 with a short blank scan to get us off on the right foot. Then we sequentially call dot rows 1 through 7 of the characters to be displayed. This live scanning is followed by a vertical sync pulse. After this, a word is loaded in the accumulator (365) that sets the number of blank scans. As many blank scans as needed are generated in turn. Each time a blank scan is completed, the accumulator word is decremented until the word hits zero. At that time, the program jumps to the top line blank scan and repeats for the next field.

Unlike a 6502, an 8080 can take an even or an odd number of *half* microseconds to complete an instruction. In most scan programs, some equalization will be needed to make up for this half-micro-second jitter. The command MOVAA or "move the accumulator to itself" takes 2.5 microseconds and is a benign instruction. This lets us shift timing by half a microsecond if used once and by one micro-second if used twice. This is the purpose of those strange "177" in-structions in the program.

In step 040 147, we disable the interrupts. This turns off our front panel but does so late enough that we will not lock the speaker on.

Since this code is not self-modifying, you can put it in your choice of RAM, ROM, PROM, EPROM, or E²PROM. Naturally, you'll want to check things out in RAM first before committing yourself to permanent code.

Your Turn:

Show the coding needed for 1 × 32, 1 × 64, and 1 × 80 scans

As a hint that will save you lots of trial and error or bunches of calculations, keep your blank initial scan *nine* counts short of the live scans, and keep the retrace blank scans *five* counts short of your live scans. A stationary or near-stationary hum bar is picked up by adjusting 040 134 as needed. A more obvious route to shorter scans is to simply use the 1 × 56 and load blanks as needed in unused character locations.

TV RETRACE HASSLES

Calling and returning from a subroutine takes around 13.5 micro-seconds on a typical 8080. Two of these microseconds are spent on the live scan, leaving us with a retrace time of 11.5 microseconds. Since the H8 is slightly faster than this, our available retrace time is something like 11.2 microseconds.

Naturally, we would like to keep our retrace times as short as pos-sible. This lets us put more characters on the line for standard hori-zontal rates, or lets us run long character lines with more nearly nor-mal horizontal frequencies.

But eleven microseconds may not be enough time for your monitor or tv set to get cleanly from the end of one line to the beginning of the next. For most monitors and some tv sets, this eleven microsec-onds will be just barely enough.

If you are having trouble displaying all the characters, here are some options that may help you:

μP—8080A		Start—JMP 040 100			Displayed 340 004 to 340 037	
System—H8		End—RST/0			342 004 to 342 037	
					Program Space 040 100 to 040 152	
					(43 words)	

```
START ──────► 040 100   CALL    315 017 140       Do short blank scan
          │   040 103   CALL    315 004 160       Scan dot row #1
          │   040 106   CALL    315 004 200       Scan dot row #2
          │   040 111   CALL    315 004 220       Scan dot row #3
          │
          │   040 114   CALL    315 004 240       Scan dot row #4
          │   040 117   CALL    315 004 260       Scan dot row #5
          │   040 122   CALL    315 004 300       Scan dot row #6
          │   040 125   CALL    315 004 320       Scan dot row #7
          │
          │   040 130   LDA     072 000 340       Output vertical sync pulse
          │   040 133   MVIA    076 365           Load # of blank scans
        ┌─040 135   CALL    315 011 140       Do blank scan
        │ │ 040 140   DCRA    075               One less scan
        ↑ │
        │ │ 040 141   MOVAA   177               Equalize 2.5 microseconds
        └─040 142   JNZ     302 (135)(040)    One more blank scan?
          │ 040 145   MOVAA   177               Equalize 5.0 microseconds
          │ 040 146   MOVAA   177                   continued
          │
          │ 040 147   DI      363               Shut off horn
          └─040 150   JMP     303 (100)(040)    Go to live scans
```

Notes:

TVT 6⅝ must be connected via an 8080 adaptor, and both the 658-HD8 and 658-HS64 PROMs must be in circuit for program to run.

Horizontal frequency 15.174 kHz; vertical frequency 59.97 Hz. 2500 second hum bar.

Address switches must be in "32," A5 = " +," and A4 = "A4" positions.

Character sequence goes 340 004; 342 004; 340 005; 342 005; 340 006; 342 006; 340 007...

( ) denotes an absolute address that is program location sensitive.

This program is not self-modifying and may be placed in PROM or ROM.

Mods;

To relocate display space, use program jumpers on memory card, or else change starting address of dot scans.

To put both halves of display space closer together, use A4 switching rather than A9 switching.

(Continued on next page)

Fig. 6-7. Program for a 1-line, 56-character, no-interlace raster scan.

* Your simplest out is to adjust the display centering so that the first character is always legible. Always stop short of the maximum display length as much as needed.
* Use a longer than needed character line and put permanent blanks where they are called for.
* Add equalization to lengthen each CALL sequence. While this is the obvious and cleanest route, it can add many words to a brute-force scan program.

MORE CHARACTERS

Our 1 × 56 scan has several obvious limitations. From this starting point, we'll want to add interlace, double stuffing, and lots more characters.

The optimum number of characters or chunks per line seems to be 56 for an H8 system using A9 switching for speed doubling. This

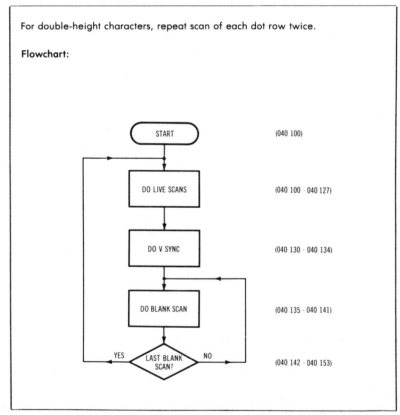

Fig. 6-7. Cont'd. Program for a 1-line, 56-character, no-interlace raster scan.

56 character length lets you use a standard horizontal frequency. You can display on either a color or a black-and-white set.

But, there seems to be something magic about 80 character lines that appeals to people, despite the fact that this many characters are hard to read and are rarely, if ever, needed. So, to prove it can be done, we're going to show you how to do 80 character lines on your H8 and then put those lines on a tv with unmodified video bandwidth or over an rf modulator. But, remember that we'll have to run at a reduced horizontal rate, which will take width and hold modifications to your small-screen, transformer-operated, PHOTOFACT-available, black-and-white set. Further, your wrong choice of set could sing objectionably.

12 LINES OF 80 CHARACTERS

A brute-force, interlaced, double-stuffed 12×80 scan program appears in Fig. 6-8. You can easily modify it for 24×80 or even 36×80 displays if you like. With the double stuffing, the 12×80 display uses slightly less than one-third of the H8 throughput time. By going to suitable transparency techniques, you can save ⅔ of the computer time to transparently run other programs such as Extended BASIC.

We've shown you this scan program with its memory space at 340 010 to 343 377. This assumes you have at least two RAM cards in your H8 and have put this particular one "out on top" with the "56K" jumper on the memory card. You may want to relocate things later, but this is a handy place to. start.

The TVT does place certain use restrictions on the 340 000 to 360 000 computer address space, since any activity here also gives you a vertical sync pulse that might disrupt an enabled display. You *can* use this space for a display memory RAM. You should *not* use this area for the scan program or the computer stack. If you do use this page for display memory RAM, you will have to watch your cursor program carefully if transparent character entry is important to you.

You'll find the 12×80 program shown in two separate fields. We have an *even* field that puts down the even dot rows of all the characters and an *odd* field that puts down the odd dot rows of all the characters. When they are combined, you end up with an interlaced and double-stuffed frame. Having the two fields separate is handy for debug. By jumping a field back on itself, you can display all-even or all-odd fields to fix coding errors or make format changes.

The scan program runs just about the same way the earlier 1×56 one did. We do a short blank scan. Then we put down the even dot rows of all the characters. Then we equalize and do a *late* vertical sync pulse, at the same time taking up one entire *extra* horizontal

µP—8080A	Start—RUN 040 100	Displayed—340 010 to 343 377
System—H8	End—RST/0	Program Space—040 100 to 042 007
		(455 words)

Even Field:

START →	040	100	CALL	315	023 140	Do short blank scan
	040	103	CALL	315	010 140	Scan dot row 0, character line 1
	040	106	CALL	315	010 200	Scan dot row 2, character line 1
	040	111	CALL	315	010 240	Scan dot row 4, character line 1
	040	114	CALL	315	010 300	Scan dot row 6, character line 1
	040	117	CALL	315	010 140	Do blank scan
	040	122	CALL	315	060 140	Scan dot row 0, character line 2
	040	125	CALL	315	060 200	Scan dot row 2, character line 2
	040	130	CALL	315	060 240	Scan dot row 4, character line 2
	040	133	CALL	315	060 300	Scan dot row 6, character line 2
	040	136	CALL	315	060 140	Do blank scan
	040	141	CALL	315	130 140	Scan dot row 0, character line 3
	040	144	CALL	315	130 200	Scan dot row 2, character line 3
	040	147	CALL	315	130 240	Scan dot row 4, character line 3
	040	152	CALL	315	130 300	Scan dot row 6, character line 3
	040	155	CALL	315	130 140	Do blank scan
	040	160	CALL	315	210 140	Scan dot row 0, character line 4
	040	163	CALL	315	210 200	Scan dot row 2, character line 4
	040	166	CALL	315	210 240	Scan dot row 4, character line 4
	040	171	CALL	315	210 300	Scan dot row 6, character line 4
	040	174	CALL	315	210 140	Do blank scan
	040	177	CALL	315	260 140	Scan dot row 0, character line 5
	040	202	CALL	315	260 200	Scan dot row 2, character line 5
	040	205	CALL	315	260 240	Scan dot row 4, character line 5
	040	210	CALL	315	260 300	Scan dot row 6, character line 5
	040	213	CALL	315	260 140	Do blank scan
	040	216	CALL	315	330 140	Scan dot row 0, character line 6
	040	221	CALL	315	330 200	Scan dot row 2, character line 6
	040	224	CALL	315	330 240	Scan dot row 4, character line 6
	040	227	CALL	315	330 300	Scan dot row 6, character line 6
	040	232	CALL	315	330 140	Do blank scan
	040	235	CALL	315	010 141	Scan dot row 0, character line 7
	040	240	CALL	315	010 201	Scan dot row 2, character line 7
	040	243	CALL	315	010 241	Scan dot row 4, character line 7
	040	246	CALL	315	010 301	Scan dot row 6, character line 7
	040	251	CALL	315	010 141	Do blank scan
	040	254	CALL	315	060 141	Scan dot row 0, character line 8
	040	257	CALL	315	060 201	Scan dot row 2, character line 8
	040	262	CALL	315	060 241	Scan dot row 4, character line 8
	040	265	CALL	315	060 301	Scan dot row 6, character line 8
	040	270	CALL	315	060 141	Do blank scan

Fig. 6-8. Program for a 12-line, 80-character-per-line,

040	273	CALL	315	130	141	Scan dot row 0, character line 9
040	276	CALL	315	130	201	Scan dot row 2, character line 9
040	301	CALL	315	130	241	Scan dot row 4, character line 9
040	304	CALL	315	130	301	Scan dot row 6, character line 9
040	307	CALL	315	130	141	Do blank scan
040	312	CALL	315	210	141	Scan dot row 0, character line 10
040	315	CALL	315	210	201	Scan dot row 2, character line 10
040	320	CALL	315	210	241	Scan dot row 4, character line 10
040	323	CALL	315	210	301	Scan dot row 6, character line 10
040	326	CALL	315	210	141	Do blank scan
040	331	CALL	315	260	141	Scan dot row 0, character line 11
040	334	CALL	315	260	201	Scan dot row 2, character line 11
040	337	CALL	315	260	241	Scan dot row 4, character line 11
040	342	CALL	315	260	301	Scan dot row 6, character line 11
040	345	CALL	315	260	141	Do blank scan
040	350	CALL	315	330	141	Scan dot row 0, character line 12
040	353	CALL	315	330	201	Scan dot row 2, character line 12
040	356	CALL	315	330	241	Scan dot row 4, character line 12
040	361	CALL	315	330	301	Scan dot row 6, character line 12
040	364	CALL	315	330	141	Do blank scan
040	367	MVIA	076	006		Delay 48.5 microseconds
040	371	DCRA	075			continued
040	372	JNZ	302	(371)	(040)	continued
040	375	LDA	072	000	340	Output //VERTICAL SYNC// pulse
041	000	CALL	315	363	140	Do short blank scan
041	003	LDA	072	000	000	Delay 6.5 microseconds
041	006	MVIA	076	175		Load # of vertical blank scans
041	010	CALL	315	015	140	Do //BLANK VERTICAL SCANS//
041	013	DCRA	075			One less blank scan
041	014	MOVAA	177			Equalize 2.5 microseconds
041	015	JNZ	302	(010)	(041)	Repeat blank scans if not done
041	020	MOVAA	177			Equalize 5 microseconds
041	021	MOVAA	177			continued
041	022	DI	363			Shut off horn
041	023	JMP	303	(100)	(041)	Jump to odd field
(041	026	to 041 077 are spares)				

Odd Field:

041	100	CALL	315	023	140	Do short blank scan
041	103	CALL	315	010	160	Scan dot row 1, character line 1
041	106	CALL	315	010	220	Scan dot row 3, character line 1
041	111	CALL	315	010	260	Scan dot row 5, character line 1
041	114	CALL	315	010	320	Scan dot row 7, character line 1
041	117	CALL	315	010	140	Do blank scan
041	122	CALL	315	060	160	Scan dot row 1, character line 2
041	125	CALL	315	060	220	Scan dot row 3, character line 2
041	130	CALL	315	060	260	Scan dot row 5, character line 2
041	133	CALL	315	060	320	Scan dot row 7, character line 2
041	136	CALL	315	060	140	Do blank scan

(Continued on next page)

full-interlace, double-stuffed TVT 6⅝ raster scan.

041	141	CALL	315	130	160	Scan dot row 1, character line 3
041	144	CALL	315	130	220	Scan dot row 3, character line 3
041	147	CALL	315	130	260	Scan dot row 5, character line 3
041	152	CALL	315	130	320	Scan dot row 7, character line 3
041	155	CALL	315	130	140	Do blank scan
041	160	CALL	315	210	160	Scan dot row 1, character line 4
041	163	CALL	315	210	220	Scan dot row 3, character line 4
041	166	CALL	315	210	260	Scan dot row 5, character line 4
041	171	CALL	315	210	320	Scan dot row 7, character line 4
041	174	CALL	315	210	140	Do blank scan
041	177	CALL	315	260	160	Scan dot row 1, character line 5
041	202	CALL	315	260	220	Scan dot row 3, character line 5
041	205	CALL	315	260	260	Scan dot row 5, character line 5
041	210	CALL	315	260	320	Scan dot row 7, character line 5
041	213	CALL	315	260	140	Do blank scan
041	216	CALL	315	330	160	Scan dot row 1, character line 6
041	221	CALL	315	330	220	Scan dot row 3, character line 6
041	224	CALL	315	330	260	Scan dot row 5, character line 6
041	227	CALL	315	330	320	Scan dot row 7, character line 6
041	232	CALL	315	330	140	Do blank scan
041	235	CALL	315	010	161	Scan dot row 1, character line 7
041	240	CALL	315	010	221	Scan dot row 3, character line 7
041	243	CALL	315	010	261	Scan dot row 5, character line 7
041	246	CALL	315	010	321	Scan dot row 7, character line 7
041	251	CALL	315	010	141	Do blank scan
041	254	CALL	315	060	161	Scan dot row 1, character line 8
041	257	CALL	315	060	221	Scan dot row 3, character line 8
041	262	CALL	315	060	261	Scan dot row 5, character line 8
041	265	CALL	315	060	321	Scan dot row 7, character line 8
041	270	CALL	315	060	141	Do blank scan
041	273	CALL	315	130	161	Scan dot row 1, character line 9
041	276	CALL	315	130	221	Scan dot row 3, character line 9
041	301	CALL	315	130	261	Scan dot row 5, character line 9
041	304	CALL	315	130	321	Scan dot row 7, character line 9
041	307	CALL	315	130	141	Do blank scan
041	312	CALL	315	210	161	Scan dot row 1, character line 10
041	315	CALL	315	210	221	Scan dot row 3, character line 10
041	320	CALL	315	210	261	Scan dot row 5, character line 10
041	323	CALL	315	210	321	Scan dot row 7, character line 10
041	326	CALL	315	210	141	Do blank scan
041	331	CALL	315	260	161	Scan dot row 1, character line 11
041	334	CALL	315	260	221	Scan dot row 3, character line 11
041	337	CALL	315	260	261	Scan dot row 5, character line 11
041	342	CALL	315	260	321	Scan dot row 7, character line 11
041	345	CALL	315	260	141	Do blank scan
041	350	CALL	315	330	161	Scan dot row 1, character line 12
041	353	CALL	315	330	221	Scan dot row 3, character line 12
041	356	CALL	315	330	261	Scan dot row 5, character line 12
041	361	CALL	315	330	321	Scan dot row 7, character line 12
041	364	CALL	315	330	141	Do blank scan

Fig. 6-8. Cont'd. Program for a 12-line, 80-character-per-

```
041  367   LDA    072 000 340    Output //VERTICAL SYNC// pulse
041  372   MVIA   076 175        Load # of vertical blank scans
041  374   CALL   315 015 140    Do //BLANK VERTICAL SCANS//
041  377   DCRA   075            One less blank scan
042  000   MOVAA  177            Equalize 2.5 microseconds
042  001   JNZ    302 (374)(041) Repeat blank scans if not done
042  004   MOVAA  177            Equalize 5 microseconds
042  005   MOVAA  177                continued
042  006   DI     363            Shut off horn
042  007   JMP    303 (100)(040)
```

Notes:

TVT 6⅝ must be connected via an 8080 adaptor, and both the 658-HD8 and 658-HS80 PROMs must be in circuit for the program to run.

Address switches must be in "64," A5 = "A5," and A4 = "A4" positions.

Horizontal frequency = 11.191 kHz. Vertical frequency = 60.006 Hz. 166 second hum bar.

This program is not self-modifying and may be placed in PROM or ROM.

Character sequence goes 340 000; 350 000; 340 001; 350 001; 340 002; 350 002; 340 003 ....

( ) denotes an absolute address that is program location sensitive.

Flowchart:

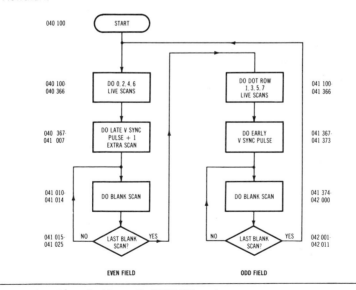

line, full-interlace, double-stuffed TVT 6⅝ raster scan.

scan time. Then we do the usual blank vertical scans, completing the field.

When the field is finished, we jump to the odd field, do a short blank scan, and then put down all the odd dot rows of all the characters. After this, we do an *early* vertical sync pulse and then go on to the usual number of vertical blank scans. The scan sequence repeats by then jumping to the start of an even field.

The early and late vertical sync pulses differ by half a horizontal line. When you combine this half a line with the *extra* horizontal line picked up only in the even scan, you end up with an interlaced scan of 373 whole lines taking one 30-hertz frame. This 30-hertz frame consists of two 60-hertz fields of 186.5 lines each.

The 658-HS80 Scan PROM lets you repack the 80 character lines so you can use your display memory space efficiently. Fig. 6-9 shows how the characters are arranged in RAM. While this looks like a royal mess, a few extra cursor words are all we need to straighten things out. This is more than a reasonable tradeoff for letting us do long lines with an 8080 in the first place and freeing up 600 or so words of system RAM for other uses.

Your Turn:

* Show the coding for 24 × 80, 32 × 80, 16 × 56, 32 × 56, 16 × 64, and 32 × 64 scan programs.

* Show ways of very much shortening the 12 × 80 scan program while staying PROM compatible. Try:
  —Using only one vertical blanking sequence, and minimizing blank sequences and unused code words.
  —Using indirect JSR commands.
  —Using I/O commands to free address space.
—Using interrupt mapping.

Note that you will use the HS64 PROM for 64 and shorter character lines and most graphics. The HS80 PROM is usually reserved for 80 character lines. You can do 40 character lines with the HS64 without any repacking, or else you can go to a specially coded HS40 PROM that uses repacking. Or, you can ultimately go the scrungy video route and eliminate all the PROMS altogether.

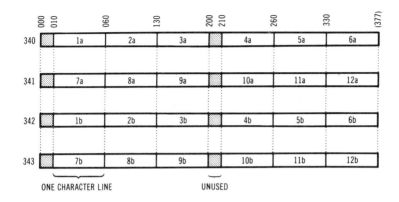

Fig. 6-9. Display memory map for 12 × 80 scan.

8080 CURSOR SOFTWARE

Many of the ideas we have already used for our previous cursors will carry over the 8080 cursor design. One new hassle we'll pick up is the straightening-out process needed to undo the A9 speed doubling. But, this is more than offset by the easier and simpler code you get by using all the available 8080 registers, particularly the 16-bit-wide HL register that is ideal for cursor location storage.

Let's look at a simple cursor that ties the keyboard input to an 8080 display. We'll use the 1 × 56 display to keep things simple. You'll find the program shown as Fig. 6-10.

For convenience, we've left this program in several pieces, omitted a visible cursor, and have done only "good enough" equalization. While you can use this program for a one-line point-of-sale terminal, as a deaf communicator, or in a prompting environment, chances are that you'll want to pick up these bits and pieces and then combine them with the best of the earlier cursors to do your own thing.

Our main scan sequence is pretty much the same as the old 1 × 56 scan program of Fig. 6-7. We've added some words at the start that initialize our H8-5 serial interface so that it will accept a keyboard input by way of the keyboard serial adaptor. Our brute-force scans are called for next, as needed to give us a line of characters.

After the characters are down, we test to see if a new key has been pressed. If not, we go on and output a vertical sync pulse, do the blank vertical retrace scans, and then jump up and repeat everything for the next field. Note that we do NOT re-initialize the serial interface each time. Instead, we simply loop back to the start of the next field.

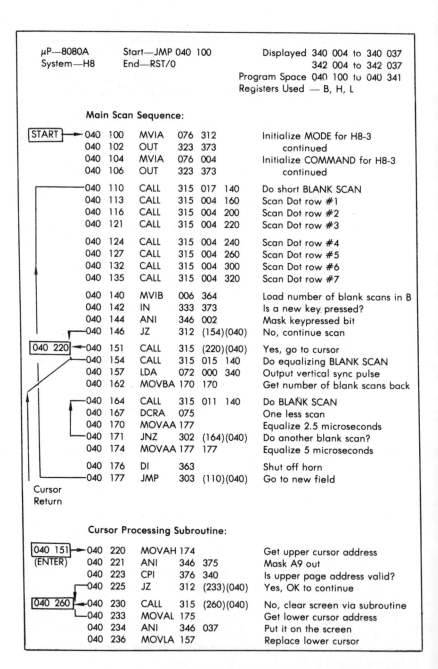

μP—8080A	Start—JMP 040 100			Displayed 340 004 to 340 037	
System—H8	End—RST/0			342 004 to 342 037	

Program Space 040 100 to 040 341
Registers Used — B, H, L

Main Scan Sequence:

START →	040	100	MVIA	076 312	Initialize MODE for H8-3
	040	102	OUT	323 373	continued
	040	104	MVIA	076 004	Initialize COMMAND for H8-3
	040	106	OUT	323 373	continued
	040	110	CALL	315 017 140	Do short BLANK SCAN
	040	113	CALL	315 004 160	Scan Dot row #1
	040	116	CALL	315 004 200	Scan Dot row #2
	040	121	CALL	315 004 220	Scan Dot row #3
	040	124	CALL	315 004 240	Scan Dot row #4
	040	127	CALL	315 004 260	Scan Dot row #5
	040	132	CALL	315 004 300	Scan Dot row #6
	040	135	CALL	315 004 320	Scan Dot row #7
	040	140	MVIB	006 364	Load number of blank scans in B
	040	142	IN	333 373	Is a new key pressed?
	040	144	ANI	346 002	Mask keypressed bit
	040	146	JZ	312 (154)(040)	No, continue scan
040 220 →	040	151	CALL	315 (220)(040)	Yes, go to cursor
	040	154	CALL	315 015 140	Do equalizing BLANK SCAN
	040	157	LDA	072 000 340	Output vertical sync pulse
	040	162	MOVBA	170 170	Get number of blank scans back
	040	164	CALL	315 011 140	Do BLANK SCAN
	040	167	DCRA	075	One less scan
	040	170	MOVAA	177	Equalize 2.5 microseconds
	040	171	JNZ	302 (164)(040)	Do another blank scan?
	040	174	MOVAA	177 177	Equalize 5 microseconds
	040	176	DI	363	Shut off horn
	040	177	JMP	303 (110)(040)	Go to new field

Cursor
Return

Cursor Processing Subroutine:

040 151 →	040	220	MOVAH	174	Get upper cursor address
(ENTER)	040	221	ANI	346 375	Mask A9 out
	040	223	CPI	376 340	Is upper page address valid?
	040	225	JZ	312 (233)(040)	Yes, OK to continue
040 260 →	040	230	CALL	315 (260)(040)	No, clear screen via subroutine
	040	233	MOVAL	175	Get lower cursor address
	040	234	ANI	346 037	Put it on the screen
	040	236	MOVLA	157	Replace lower cursor

Fig .6-10. Program for a 1-line, 56-character TVT 6⅝

	040 237	IN	333	372	Get character
	040 241	CPI	376	015	Is it Carriage Return (Erase)?
	040 243	JZ	312	(260)(040)	Yes, clear screen via subroutine
[040 300]←	040 246	CALL	315	(300)(040)	No, enter character via subroutine
	040 251	RET	311		Return to scan program

(040 251 through 040 257 are spares; not used)

[040 320]←	040 260	CALL	315	(320)(040)	Go to clear screen subroutine
	040 263	MVIB	006	331	Equalize # of blank scans remaining
[040 154]←	040 265	RET	311		Return to processing
(EXIT)					

Enter Character and Increment Subroutine:

[ENTER]→	040 300	MOVMA	167		Store character at cursor location
	040 301	MOVAH	174		Get upper cursor word
	040 302	XRI	356	002	Change address A9
	040 304	MOVHA	147		Replace upper cursor word
	040 305	ANI	346	002	Is address A9 now zero?
[EXIT 1]←	040 307	RNZ	300		No, return
	040 310	INXH	043		Yes, increment HL (cursor address)
[EXIT 2]←	040 311	RET	311		Return to processing

Clear Screen Subroutine:

[ENTER]→	040 320	LXIH	041	(004)(340)	Home cursor
	040 323	MVIA	076	040	Load space
	040 325	CALL	315	(300)(040)	Enter space via ECI subroutine
	040 330	MVIA	076	040	Is it the end of the screen?
	040 332	CMPL	275		continued ...
	040 333	JNC	302	(323)(040)	No, add more spaces
	040 336	LXIH	041	(004)(340)	Yes, home cursor
[EXIT]←	040 341	RET	311		Return to processing

Notes:
TVT 6⅝ must be connected via an 8080 adaptor, and both the 658-HD8 and 658-HS64 PROMs must be in circuit for program to run. Character entry via a keyboard, a keyboard serial adaptor, and the H8-3 serial interface card.

All characters and all control commands are entered on the screen, except for carriage return (CR), which clears the screen.

Horizontal frequency is 15.174 kHz; vertical frequency is 59.976 Hz. 2500 second hum bar.

Address switches must be in "32," A5 = " +," and A4 = "A4" positions.

Character sequence goes 340 004; 342 004; 340 005; 342 005; 340 006; 342 006; 340 007 ....

8080 raster scan with integrated minimum cursor.

Now, if a key has been pressed, we jump to the new *Cursor Processing* subroutine at 040 220 through 040 251. This cursor processing subroutine first checks to make sure the HL register is holding a valid cursor location. If it isn't, the screen is erased and the cursor fixed before anything ungood is allowed to happen to other programs in the machine.

We then get a character and test it to see if it is a CR, or carriage return. If it is a CR, we erase the screen and home the cursor. CR was chosen over CAN in this example as it seems more appropriate for a one-line display. You can, of course, use any decoding you like.

This program is not self-modifying and may be placed in PROM or ROM. Register "B" is used for temporary storage; registers "HL" are used to hold the cursor address.

To shorten number of characters displayed for a tv with limited width, use 040 337 value of 005 or higher.

( ) denotes an absolute address that is program location sensitive.

Flowchart:

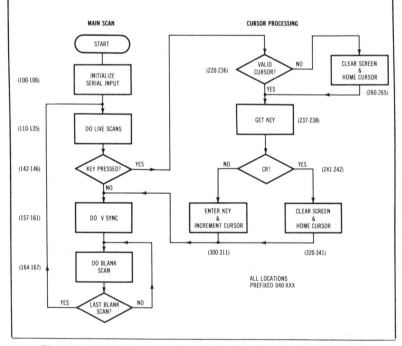

Fig. 6-10. Cont'd. Program for a 1-line, 56-character TVT 6⅝ 8080 raster scan with integrated minimum cursor.

If any key *but* the carriage return was pressed, the character gets entered. This is done by way of an enter-character-and-increment or *ECI Subroutine*. This ECI subroutine is somewhat fancier than the ones we used before, since we have the A9 switching to contend with. Some new rules and a few extra code words take care of this for us.

Remember that the A9 switching was used to let us get characters out of the 8080 fast enough to be useful. To do this, the display characters are out of order. Specifically, for our 1 × 56 display, the character sequence goes like this:

1st character	340 004
2nd character	342 004
3rd character	340 005
4th character	342 005
. . . . . .	
55th character	340 037
56th character	342 037

Now, every time we enter a character, we want to go on to the next one. So, we first *change* A9. To do this, we use an Exclusive OR 002 of the H register. This will automatically make A9 a one for a particular character, a zero for the next character, and a one for yet the next character, and so on.

If A9 goes from a zero to a one, we need do nothing further. But, if A9 goes from a one to a zero, we need to move onto the next pair of character slots in memory. To do this, we increment the HL register which contains the cursor.

So, we change A9 *every* new character but increment our HL cursor only every *second* character. And, all the A9 switching mess gets magically eliminated with nothing but eight or so program words.

Your Turn:

> Show an all-the-bells-and-whistles cursor for a 24 × 80 display, including a visible cursor, full equalization and transparency, all cursor motions, and the usual goodies.

As with the 6502 systems, there is virtually no limit to how fancy your cursor programs can get. All it takes are extra words of machine language code to do most anything you can dream up.

CHAPTER 7

Lower-Case Hardware
For Your Apple II

With a few simple modifications and some new software, you can plug a TVT 6⅝ Lower Case Module "A" into an Apple II.

These simple changes turn your Apple II into a combined upper- and lower-case computer and can cost you as little as $10. Your new lower-case ability frees up your Apple to do things like word processing, text editing, typesetting, generating mailing lists, writing form letters, and so on. The modifications take two extra integrated circuits added to the "breadboard" area already on the Apple. If you like, you can get by with only add-on wires and no foil cuts.

The change-only-the-character-generator approach doesn't tie up or restrict blocks of ROM, RAM, or graphics display memory. What we are about to show you is also totally invisible—your Apple II stays an upper-case machine until you specifically ask for some lower-case output. Software does the switchover at any time, and the regular Apple II keyboard is used for both upper and lower case.

There are two minor limitations to this conversion. If you still want to be able to reverse video, you may have to add a changeover switch that gives you a choice of reverse video *or* lower case. You'll also find that lower-case characters will be more attractively flashed with software rather than hardware. The method we'll show you should work on many other terminals and computers, if they use a new style 2513 character generator and have a full 8-bit-wide display memory.

SOME DETAILS

Just adding lower case to any old computer or terminal sounds simple enough. Plug in an upper- and lower-case combined character generator, and you are home free, right?

Well, not really. First and foremost, you have to want to do something useful with your new lower-case characters. While they are nice to look at for displays and some games, unless you have a printer or other output that needs and uses lower case, you really haven't gained very much. If you want the new characters, make sure you have some way to get them out of the machine. So, an important rule is to *make sure you have some use for lower case before you go to the trouble of providing it.*

An obvious problem that immediately crops up is the keyboard and its encoder electronics. The Apple II has an upper-case-only keyboard. They used an old National chip for the encoder. This chip is strictly upper case only, compared to the usual 2376 with its choice of coding options. The Apple keycaps, particularly those on the "M'" and the "P," will also limit how you can use the existing keyboard. And there are no spare keys to speak of.

We'll show you how to use software to trick the existing Apple II keyboard into giving us lower case when and where we want it. The software secret is to use the *Escape* key as a shift lock for lower case. More on this later.

Another problem is created by the firmware in the Apple II. The operating systems and monitor are needed for machine language, the miniassembler, for Integer BASIC, and for APPLESOFT.

All four of these languages *demand* upper case only. And the firmware is happy to provide it. In fact, most of the sequences go to a lot of trouble to make sure that everything is upper case. Put in lower case, and the sequences will convert it back for you. Even the winking cursor forces an upper-case-only output. So, even if you force feed your Apple from a new lower-case keyboard, the internal firmware will try to change it all back to upper case anyway.

The way around all this is to use some new software that bypasses the firmware when and if we need lower case. This is a key to full alphanumerics. We have to make sure that everything we do stays fully invisible and appears to be upper case only, unless we specifically call for the new characters.

Our modifications meet these goals:

* The existing keyboard is used without any changes.
* Apple hardware changes consist of two new integrated circuits in the breadboard area, and a plug-in module. No foil cuts are needed.

* Lower case is completely invisible until it is called with software.
* No hi-res graphics or large blocks of ROM or RAM are tied up.

Let's see just how we can go about all this. Fig. 7-1 shows the old and the new bit assignments for the Apple II display memory, or "DL" bus. The lower six bits (DL0–DL5) are used for the ASCII character code, arranged in the usual order. The next bit is DL6. It's used to flash the screen. Screen flashing is most often used for the cursor, but it is also handy for alarm or error messages.

The final bit is DL7. It was originally used to reverse the screen display. This gives you black characters on a white background, and is normally used for emphasis.

Lines DL6 and DL7 are not independent. You cannot flash a white screen. You can only flash a black screen. The truth table (before modification) for these two lines looks like this:

DL7	DL6	Screen
0	0	Black characters, white background
0	1	Flashing character, black background
1	0	White character, black background
1	1	White character, black background

If it weren't for the interaction between these two bits, some capital letters would always flash with the existing Apple II firmware.

The obvious thing to do is make DL7 equal to the seventh ASCII line needed for your new character generator. But there doesn't seem

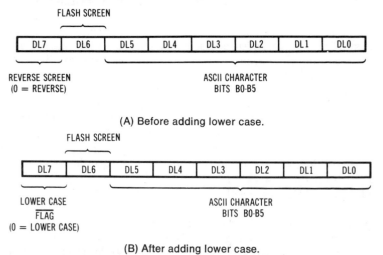

(A) Before adding lower case.

(B) After adding lower case.

Fig. 7-1. Bit definitions of Apple II character "DL" bus.

to be any reasonable way to do this and still have invisible operation when you *don't* want lower case. Instead, we use DL7 as a lower-case flag. If DL7 is a 0 *AND* if DL6 is a 0, then we want lower case out of our character generator. Otherwise, we want everything to stay just the way it was. Our new truth table looks like this:

DL7	DL6	Screen
0	0	White lower-case characters
0	1	Flashing characters
1	0	White upper-case characters
1	1	White upper-case characters

Once again, the reason we do this in a nonobvious and seemingly complicated way is to keep compatibility with everything that is already working in your Apple II.

The hardware modifications involved are simple and cheap, but you should not attempt them if you aren't good at adding wires to a printed circuit board, reading socket pins, and so on. There are three things involved in the hardware changes:

* The character generator is replaced with one that also generates lower case.
* A new integrated-circuit gate is added to decode lower case for the character generator.
* A new integrated-circuit gate is added to prevent lower-case characters from appearing as black on white.

The first change is done using a TVT 6⅝ Module "A." This consists of an $8 upper-and-lower-case Motorola MCM6674 character generator mounted on a small adaptor card that plugs into the existing 2513 character-generator socket. The second two changes involve 15¢ integrated circuits added on new sockets in the Apple breadboard area. One direct IC-to-IC wire is used to eliminate the need for any foil cuts.

The schematic of the lower-case modification for the Apple II is shown in Fig. 7-2. Character generator A5 is unplugged and replaced with a TVT Module "A" that carries a new upper-and-lower-case MCM6674P character generator. A new wire routed to pin 23 of A5 carries the new seventh ASCII bit, A6, needed for the dual-case operation.

The logic rules for this new lead tell us to make A6 the complement of A5 for upper case, numerals, and punctuation, but to make A6 a "1" for lower case. This lower-case condition happens when DL6 and DL7 are both zeros.

A new 74LS02 quad NOR gate integrated circuit is put in the breadboard area at A11 to do this A6 logic conversion for us. The

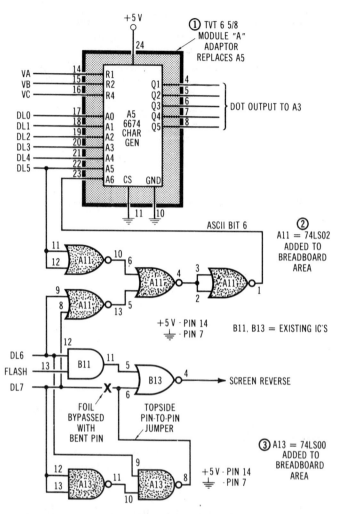

Fig. 7-2. Schematic of Apple II lower-case modifications.

gate outputs a "1" if DL6 and DL7 are both "0," and otherwise outputs the complement of DL5. The reasons behind this logic are apparent if you study the ASCII coding involved.

If we simply changed the character generator and added a quad NOR gate, we would get invisible normal operation and lower case when we called for it. The only hassle involved is that the lower case would appear as reverse video, with black characters on a white background. To beat this final problem, we add a second integrated circuit in the breadboard area. A13 outputs a signal for us that is

DO NOT PLUG AN UNMODIFIED TVT MODULE "A" INTO AN UNMODIFIED APPLE II!

INSTEAD ...
* Leave pins 1 and 12 off Module "A" during assembly

... or ...

* Bend pins 1 and 12 of Module "A" up and out of the road

... or ...

* Cut pins 1 and 12 of Module "A" flush with its circuit board

... or ...

* Use a PC layout for Module "A" that floats pins 1 and 12

... or ...

* Cut the foil on the dead-end supply lines going to pins 1 and 12 of character generator A5 on your Apple II.

Fig. 7-3. Several routes to module "A" compatibility with Apple II.

low only when the flashing condition of DL6 = 1 and DL7 = 0 takes place. Otherwise, a "1" is output and forces the normal white-on-black screen display.

Note that the original DL7 connection going to pin 6 of B13 has to somehow be broken. This can be done by cutting foil, but a safer and more reversible way is to bend pin 6 of B13 out of its socket, and make a direct topside wire connection.

There is one final detail we must attend to in the modification for lower case. The Apple II still applies unused negative voltages to pins 1 and 12 of the character generator. This probably dates from the days when some 2513's needed these supply voltages, or else it is a hedge should a different part be needed. At any rate, **an unmodified TVT Module "A" will short out the power supplies if it is plugged into an unmodified Apple II!** Fig. 7-3 shows several ways out of this bind. Anything that keeps a short off the −5-volt and −12-volt lines will work.

HARDWARE CHANGES

As with just about anything in the new computer world, there's both hardware and software involved. If you make only the hardware changes we are about to look at, your Apple II will still behave just like it did before, with the only exception being the loss of screen reversal. To actually use lower case, we have to add new software as well.

Our new software examples will be in the form of short integer BASIC programs and sequences. Once you decide what you really want to do with your lower-case Apple, you can use these sequences as they are, can integrate them into your working programs, or can convert them up to APPLESOFT or down to machine language. We'll be giving you more than enough software to get you started.

Fig. 7-4 repeats the details of the TVT Module "A" from *The Cheap Video Cookbook* (Sams Catalog No. 21524). We have changed the callouts around to match the Apple's and have eliminated pins 1 and 12 from the module to eliminate the supply shorting problem.

Assembly of your Module "A" goes like this:

( ) Carefully inspect the circuit board for opens, solder bridges, etc. Try tinning one of the runs on the board. If there is any problem with easy solder adhesion, carefully clean all the areas to be soldered with an ordinary pink eraser. Avoid handling the board, as it will make soldering more difficult.

( ) Set your PC board bare side up with the notch in the upper left-hand corner. Insert a 0.1-μF disc ceramic capacitor in the two middle, left-most holes. Solder the capacitor in place. Clip and save the excess leads.

( ) Use one of the leads left over from the previous step to provide a jumper in the two middle, right-most holes.

( ) Use the other remaining lead to provide a jumper immediately to the left of the one you just installed. Solder both jumpers in place.

( ) Add an 18-pin integrated circuit to the remaining middle holes. If the socket has orientation marks or notches on it, point these toward the capacitor.

( ) Shorten one of the 12-pin strips so that it is only 10 pins long. Center this strip above the socket. The long end of the pins and the spacer go on the bare side; the short pin side goes to the foil. Solder in place after making sure that the strip is flat and that one hole remains unused at each end of the strip.

( ) Add a 12-pin strip to the remaining 12 holes at the bottom. Be sure this strip is flat before soldering and that it points the same direction as the previous strip.

( ) Carefully study Fig. 7-4D, and add the following four wire-pencil connections to the FOIL SIDE:
    ( ) IC pin 12 to module pin 4
    ( ) IC pin 13 to module pin 5

(   ) IC pin 15 to module pin 7
(   ) IC pin 16 to module pin 8

NOTE: Be sure you understand the pin numbering before you start. On the foil side, the connector pins run *counter-clockwise*. The pins on the 18-pin IC socket run *clockwise*. The end jumper and capacitor holes are *not* counted. There are no module pins at locations 1 and 12.

(   ) Check the previous step. Your four connections should form a "cross within a cross" that reverses the sequence of five side-by-side pad pairs.

(   ) Insert a *Motorola* MCM6674P character generator into the module, **putting the notch at the capacitor end.** You may have to gently force the pins slightly together by rotating the IC against a table top or bench.

(   ) Store your completed module in protective foam.

This completes assembly of your Module "A."

Chart 7-1. What You Will Need to Add Lower Case to an Apple II

Parts:
1 — TVT Module "A" lower case plug-in with floating pins 1 and 12 (Fig. 7-4)
2 — 14-pin integrated-circuit sockets
1 — 74LS02 quad low-power Schottky TTL NOR gate
1 — 74LS00 quad low-power Schottky TTL NAND gate
1 — Length of #24 solid, insulated wire, around two feet long
1 — Length of electronic solder suitable for PC board use, around two feet long

Tools:
Phillips screwdriver
¼" nutdriver (optional)
Needle-nose pliers
Diagonal cutting pliers
Wire stripper
Small soldering iron

Chart 7-1 gives a list of the tools and parts you will need for your Apple II modifications. If you know how to solder on a printed-circuit board, and are familiar with PC socket numbering, the changes should be cheap and easy to do. If you aren't into this sort of thing, or if chopping and channelling a $1000 computer is against your religious convictions, have somebody else do the work for you.

Your conversion can go like this:

(   ) Turn your Apple II off and remove supply power. Remove all video cables the line cord, and all cassette cables.

Upper– and Lower–Case

Parts List

1—MCM6674 Character Generator (Motorola)
1—18-pin low-profile IC socket
1—0.1-μF disc ceramic capacitor
2—12-pin strips (AMP 1-640098-2)
1—circuit board "A"
2—jumpers made from capacitor leads
4—jumpers made with wiring pencil
—solder

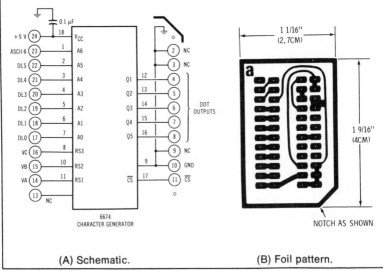

(A) Schematic.   (B) Foil pattern.

Fig. 7-4. Construction

Alphanumeric Module

How It Works

ASCII code is input on pins A0 through A6. R1, R2, and R4 row commands are input from Apple VA, VB, and VC timing. Dot matrix code is output to video shift register at Q1 through Q5. Chip select is permanently enabled. Cursor winking is external and done by software or reversing video after serial conversion.

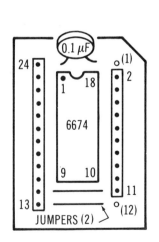

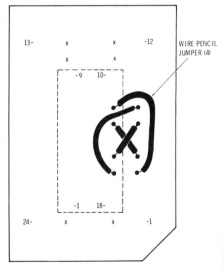

(C) Pin side.   (D) Foil side.

details of module "A."

( ) Lift the lid of the Apple II. You do this by pulling sharply up first left of rear center and then right of rear center to snap the Hedlok fasteners. Set the lid aside.

( ) Carefully unplug any remaining rf modulator cables, game paddles, other I/O connections, and any plug-in cards, making a careful note of where they go and how they are oriented.

( ) Place the Apple II upside down on a bench that is covered with a rug or a foam pad.

( ) Remove the four semirecessed Phillips-head screws at the bottom front (Fig. 7-5). Set them aside in a safe place.

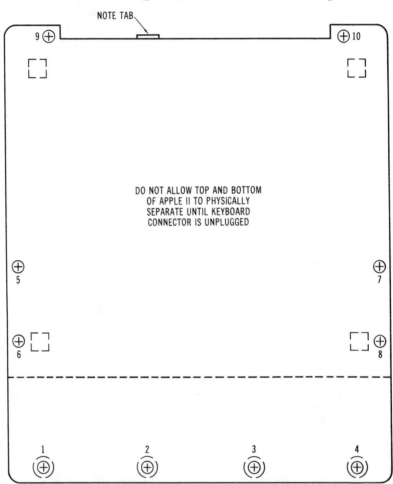

Fig. 7-5. To disassemble your Apple II, remove only the screws shown here.

( ) Remove only the six *outermost* Phillips-head screws from the bottom (Fig. 7-5). There should be two at extreme left, two at extreme right, and two at extreme rear. Set these screws aside. **Do not remove any other screws!** The outside six screws may be a slightly different color than the others.

( ) While you are carefully holding the top and bottom of the computer **tightly** together, turn the computer over so that it is right side up.

( ) **Gently** lift up the front of the computer only far enough that you can see inside. Note the keyboard connector that plugs into location A7. Gently remove this connector from the main computer board end.

( ) Check the rear of the main circuit board by the VIDEO jack. If an rf modulator or something else is plugged into the four-pin connector at K14, carefully remove it.

( ) At this point there should be nothing preventing you from removing the top of the case. Remove the cover and set it aside.

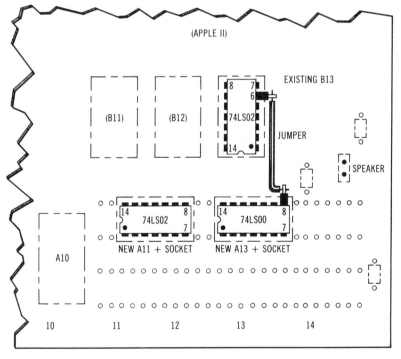

Fig. 7-6. Topside pictorial of lower-case modifications. Jumper shown eliminates need for foil cut.

> **Important Note:** The pins on the keyboard connector and the unprotected speaker cone are easily damaged. Be gentle!

( ) Note how the integrated circuits are numbered by column and alphabetized by row. Verify that
      ( ) There is a 2513 character generator at A5
      ( ) There is a breadboard area at A11 through A14
      ( ) All integrated circuits have code notches and dots that line up pin 1 with white dots on the board.
( ) Unplug the power supply connector. Pry gently against the plastic clips on either end of the socket to release them.
( ) Remove the 6-32 nut and washer in the center of the main computer board near F8.
( ) Unplug the speaker connector.
( ) Note there are six white nylon board supports. Be sure to note the one at J9.
( ) Gently squeeze the support at A1 with your needle-nose pliers until the barb releases the board. Lift the board up only far enough to free it from the barb.
( ) Release the other barbs, one at a time, starting with A14, followed by J9, K14, K9, and finally K1.
( ) Remove the circuit board from the computer. Set all the computer parts aside except for the circuit board.
( ) Study Fig. 7-6. Add a 14-pin integrated-circuit socket to A11, so that it straddles the uppermost breadboard row, starts in the *third* hole from the left (two holes show at socket left) and has any notches or dots oriented to the left. Tack the IC socket in place at pins 1 and 8. Then remelt these pins while pushing down on the socket to make sure it is solidly seated. Solder all 14 pins from the foil side.
( ) Skip two holes and add a second 14-pin integrated-circuit socket immediately to the right of the first one. It should also straddle the upper two rows and should have seven holes visible on the right and two holes visible between the sockets.
( ) Plug a 74LS02 into the left-most socket at A11, making sure the code dot and notch go to the left as shown.
( ) Take a 74LS00 and carefully bend pin 8 that so it sticks straight out. Now plug this 74LS00 into location A13, making sure the code dot and notch go to the left as shown.
( ) Carefully remove the 74LS02 in socket B13. Then bend pin 6 of this integrated circuit straight out. Replace this integrated circuit in its socket, making sure the code notch and

dot point down toward you, just like all the others in that row.

( ) Prepare a 1¼-inch (32 mm) wire by stripping ⅛ inch (3 mm) of insulation from each end. This should be a solid wire, preferably #24.

( ) Solder this wire between the two "flying" pins, pin 8 of A13 and pin 6 of B13.

( ) Turn the board upside down and provide the following connections, each time picking a reasonable length of wire and stripping ⅛ inch (3 mm) from each end. When soldering to existing pads, butt the wire against the pad after tinning it. Do not place the wire beside the pad where it can contact the next pad over. **Note that integrated-circuit pins count** *clockwise* **from the foil side.** See Fig. 7-7.

>( ) Ground wire 7/A11 to 7/A13 to ground at green capacitor A14. **Do not connect to the wide foil.** Connect only to the capacitor lead.

>( ) +5-V supply wire 14/A11 to 14/A13 to +5 at green capacitor A14. **Do connect to wide foil.**

>( ) ASCII bit 6 output wire 23/A5 to 1/A11.

>( ) Short bare jumper 2/A11 to 3/A11 to 4/A11.

>( ) Short bare jumper 5/A11 to 13/A11.

>( ) Short bare jumper 6/A11 to 10/A11.

>( ) DL5 input wire from 22/A5 to 11/A11 and 12/A11.

>( ) DL6 from 5/B8 to 9/A11 to 9/A13. Be very careful finding 5/B8. Note the square foil pad on all pin #1's of the integrated circuits.

( ) DL7 from 7/B8 to 8/A11 to 13/A13 and 12/A13.

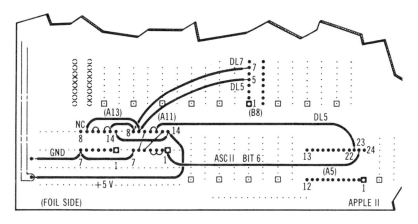

Fig. 7-7. Bottom-side pictorial of lower-case modifications.

185

(   ) Short bare jumper 10/A13 to 11/A13.

(   ) Inspect all the previous connections for possible shorts against adjacent pins.

(   ) Remove character generator A5 from the computer and store it in protective foam. If you have no other foam, use the other side of the foam holding module "A."

(   ) Plug module "A" into A5 so that the notched corner is located at A4. See Fig. 7-8.

(APPLE II)

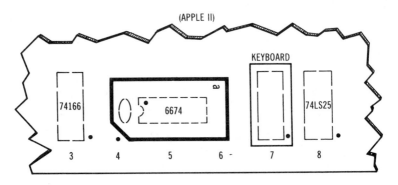

Fig. 7-8. Correct positioning of module "A."

(   ) Vigorously shake the board to make sure no wire ends remain on the board. This completes the actual modifications.

(   ) Gently place the board back onto the nylon supports on the computer bottom. Press down until each barb grabs its portion of the circuit board.

(   ) Replace the 6-32 washer and nut in the center of the board.

(   ) Plug the power supply connector and the speaker back into their respective sockets.

(   ) Set the top back onto the computer.

(   ) Gently lift the top and plug in the keyboard connector at location A7, KEYBOARD. Make sure that pin 1 aligns with the white dot and that no pins are bent, and that no pins stick out either end of the socket. Check the keyboard end of this ribbon cable to make sure it is also firmly seated.

(   ) Reconnect the rf modulator to the 4-pin VIDEO connector if you have one.

(   ) While you are firmly holding the top and bottom of your computer together, carefully turn it upside down onto the rug or foam pad on your bench.

(   ) There is a metal hook at the back of the computer. Make sure this hook goes into its matching slot in the plastic top (Fig. 7-5).

( ) Replace the rearmost two Phillips screws. Do not tighten completely. Note that these are flathead screws without washers.
( ) Replace the center front two Phillips screws. Do not tighten completely. Note that these are binder head screws with lock washers.
( ) Replace the remaining two binder head screws at the front.
( ) Replace the remaining four flathead screws, two on each side.
( ) Tighten all screws.
( ) Replace the game paddles, rf output leads, I/O cards, and I/O connectors, exactly as you found them.
( ) Replace the cover. Tuck the front end under the top of the computer and then carefully align the cover. Then press firmly down with the heel of your hand, first at left rear, then at right rear, until the Hedlock fasteners snap into place.
( ) Replace the video and cassette connectors and line cord.

This completes the modification of your Apple II to lower case.

INITIAL CHECKOUT

Here's how to check your modification to make sure it is working:

( ) Switch the computer to off and then plug it in.
( ) Very briefly switch the computer on and then back off again. The power supply should click only once, and the POWER light should come on. If the power supply continuously clicks or if the POWER light doesn't come on, you have a short somewhere. Backtrack and find out where.
( ) Now switch the computer on only long enough to press the RESET key. The speaker should beep. If the speaker does not beep, STOP and find out why.
( ) Check out your display with an integer BASIC program of some sort. You should have a completely normal display, all upper case and white on a black background. Some of the punctuation may be slightly different, such as larger periods and commas.
( ) Look ahead and load the integer BASIC program of Fig. 8-4. RUN this program. All the letters should appear as lower case on the lower line, repeating over and over again. Numerals and punctuation should appear normally. As this is a simple test program used for debugging, don't worry about things like the missing cursor and the lack of scrolling.

( ) Type a CTRL "A." You should get a capital letter A. Type a CTRL "B." You should get a capital B.

( ) Type a CTRL "C." What happens? Why?

Your Turn:

Why doesn't the Apple like to display a capital "C" when you hit CTRL-C?

This completes your checkout. Should you have problems, isolate the trouble to the likely area. For instance, if you can't light the POWER lamp or if the power supply continuously clicks, look for shorts caused by not floating pins 1 and 12 of module "A," solder blobs or two-pad shorts, or integrated circuits plugged in wrong. Note that an *unconnected* power supply will also continuously click.

Your module "A" generates the characters for you. It receives its lower-case control signal from A11. The screen-reversal inhibiting is done by A13. Should anything in the way of hassles show up, isolate things to the source.

If you want to get back to upper case only, just put the old character generator back, remove A11, A13, and B13, and then put the new 74LS02 back in slot B13. If you are an old pro at PC work, you can put the topside wire on the bottom by cutting the foil going to pin 6 of B13. This is not recommended until after you have debugged your lower case.

Later, we'll see how you can add a switch to give you a choice of reverse screen or lower case.

If you are going to do anything useful with your lower case, you'll have to add some software that calls for the lower case when it is needed. Let's turn to the software development next.

CHAPTER **8**

Lower-Case Software
For Your Apple II

Your Apple II hardware mods of the last chapter will do nothing
for you until you add some lower-case software to activate the new
hardware. How much you need in the way of software depends on
what you want to do with your new lower-case ability. If you are
only going to use lower case for annotation of a game here or there,
very little new will be needed. Most likely, your lower-case software
will have to interact with any floppy discs or printers you have on-
line, and you'll want an extensive editing capability. So, let's look
at three different levels of software involvement. First, we'll use the
absolute minimum we need to get anything lower case at all on the
screen. Then, we'll show you something that lets you fill the screen
with mixed upper and lower case and provides a working carriage
return, scroll, and so on. Finally, we'll check into a heavyweight full
lower-case editing program that lets you put any character you want
anywhere on the screen, without the prompts and with full and easy
editing. From here on, you'll be on your own to interact with what
you really want to do with your new lower-case ability.

We will use Integer BASIC for our software. This is easy but
risky. Cursor and entry programs are best written in machine language, since they can be very fast and very efficient when done this
way. Integer BASIC *may* end up too slow for some things, particularly for repeatedly inserting and deleting characters. But Integer
BASIC is very flexible and very easy to use. It's also very easy to

change. So, we'll use the Integer BASIC route. If things turn out a bit slow, we can pull some of the stunts in the green Apple book to speed things up. Or, once you know exactly what you want, you can go the machine language route.

We will note in passing that there are simple and elegant machine-language cursor and entry manipulations already in the Apple monitor. These are available for call to an Integer BASIC program. But, many of these sequences *demand* upper case only and are restrictive in how you access them. So, we will avoid using what is already on hand—unless these sequences clearly and simply speed things up for us without creating more hassles than they solve.

Lower Case:

32	33	34	35	36	37	38	39	40	41	42	43	44	45	46	47
\	a	b	c	d	e	f	g	h	i	j	k	l	m	n	o

48	49	50	51	52	53	54	55	56	57	58	59	60	61	62	63
p	q	r	s	t	u	v	w	x	y	z	{	|	}	~	:::

CURSOR ⟶ ◢

Upper Case:

128	129	130	131	132	133	134	135	136	137	138	139	140	141	142	143
@	A	B	C	D	E	F	G	H	I	J	K	L	M	N	O

144	145	146	147	148	149	150	151	152	153	154	155	156	157	158	159
P	Q	R	S	T	U	V	W	X	Y	Z	[	\	]	↑	—

Numerals:

160	161	162	163	164	165	166	167	168	169	170	171	172	173	174	175
spc	!	"	#	$	%	&	'	(	)	*	+	,	—	`	/

176	177	178	179	180	181	182	183	184	185	186	187	188	189	190	191
0	1	2	3	4	5	6	7	8	9	:	;	<	=	>	?

Use software only to flash lower case.

To flash upper case or numerals, subtract 64 from decimal value or use software.

Decimal numbers not shown are redundant.

Fig. 8-1. The decimal character codes needed for direct POKEing into display memory.

DIRECT ENTRY

The minimum software route to displaying lower case is to simply POKE the value of the character into the place you want it to go on the screen. This is very limited if you want to put down more than a few characters at once.

We'll shortly see what the decimal memory locations of every point on the display are. For instance, we'll find out that the bottom line of the screen goes from decimal 2000 at the left to decimal 2039 at the right.

Fig. 8-1 shows the correct character codes for all the characters *as they are to be stored in memory.* For instance, say you want to put a character on the bottom line, third from the left. For an upper-case "A," use POKE 2002, 129. For a lower-case "a," use POKE 2002, 33, and so on.

The missing numbers in Fig. 8-1 are repeats of the characters already shown. A POKE in the range of 64 to 127 will flash an *upper case* character or letter. I haven't found a good hardware way to flash lower case, so we will use software for flashing or winking cursors. More on this later.

FOUR UTILITY SEQUENCES

It's far more desirable to get your characters from the keyboard than to extract them from memory or use POKE commands. Before we look at the lower-case keyboard entry stuff, let's pick up some Integer BASIC utility sequences that may be very handy for us. Four of these sequences are shown in Fig. 8-2.

First, and most important, we have to be able to read the keyboard without using a carriage return for every character. Fig. 8-2A shows how to do this. The Apple II keyboard is located at decimal −16384. If a key is pressed, the number at this location will exceed decimal 127, and the value will correspond to the selected key.

We'll call the look at the keyboard CHAR, short for *character.* We keep looking at the keyboard with the PEEK command. If we ever get a CHAR that is more than 127, this means a key has been pressed, so we save the value of CHAR. Then we reset the keyboard strobe with the POKE (−16368), 0 command shown. Be sure to always reset the keyboard after you read it. Your value for CHAR is the decimal equivalent of the pressed key. It can be used in the next step of your program or saved until needed. After you are done with this particular key, jump to 200 to await a new closure.

You can print the decimal values of all the keys simply by adding a PRINT CHAR command (Fig. 8-2B). This will display the value of each key as it is pressed. The results of this for all the keys are

A. TO READ THE KEYBOARD:

```
200 CHAR = PEEK (−16384): IF CHAR < 127 THEN 200:
    POKE (−16368),0
```

This sequence stays at 200 until a key is pressed. Key value before strobe reset appears as CHAR.

B. TO PRINT THE DECIMAL VALUE OF A PRESSED KEY:

```
200 CHAR = PEEK (−16384): IF CHAR < 127 THEN 200:
    POKE (−16368),0: PRINT CHAR: GOTO 200
```

This sequence stays at 200 until a key is pressed. Key decimal value is displayed for each new key pressed. CTRL C stops the action.

C. TO STOP A PROGRAM WITHOUT SCROLLING OR PROMPTING:

```
600 GOTO 600
```

This trap holds the screen and prevents scrolling or prompting. To get out of the trap, use CTRL C.

D. TO MEASURE THE SPEED OF AN INTEGER BASIC SEQUENCE:

```
100 FOR N = 1 TO 10000
200 (((((SEQUENCE GOES HERE)))))
300 NEXT N
```

The execution time in *milliseconds* equals *one-tenth* the number of *seconds* from RUN until the speaker beeps, minus the time (about 1 millisecond) to run with no step 200.

Fig. 8-2. Some Integer BASIC utility sequences for the Apple II.

shown you in Fig. 8-3. You'll find this chart handy to decode the various control functions. We see that the Apple II keyboard has no apparent way to provide lower-case characters, as well as the upper-case \ and [. Control characters NUL, FS, GS, RS, and US are also not immediately available. Upper case] is hidden as a shifted M and is used as the APPLESOFT prompt.

One of the more infuriating things that happens when you are building a display editing program is that you put something somewhere, and then the BASIC throws in a scroll and a prompt, moving everything up screen. To temporarily defeat the return to BASIC, just use a trap like the 600 GOTO 600 shown in Fig. 8-2C. Your program will stick in the trap until you release it. This gives you the chance to watch part of a program to make sure it is doing what you want it to. To release your trap, use CTRL C. You must, of course, eliminate all traps from your final program.

NORMAL	SHIFT	CTRL
1 (177)	! (161)	1 (177)
2 (178)	" (162)	2 (178)
3 (179)	# (163)	3 (179)
4 (180)	$ (164)	4 (180)
5 (181)	% (165)	5 (181)
6 (182)	& (166)	6 (182)
7 (183)	' (167)	7 (183)
8 (184)	((168)	8 (184)
9 (185)	) (169)	9 (185)
0 (176)	0 (176)	0 (176)
: (186)	* (170)	: (186)
−(173)	= (189)	−(173)
ESC (155)	ESC (155)	ESC (155)
Q (209)	Q (209)	DC1 (145)
W (215)	W (215)	ETB (151)
E (197)	E (197)	ENQ (133)
R (210)	R (210)	DC2 (146)
T (212)	T (212)	DC4 (148)
Y (217)	Y (217)	EM (153)
U (213)	U (213)	NAK (149)
I (201)	I (201)	HT (137)
O (207)	O (207)	SI (143)
P (208)	@ (192)	DLE (144)
CR (141)	CR (141)	CR (141)

NORMAL	SHIFT	CTRL
A (193)	A (193)	SOH (129)
S (211)	S (211)	DC3 (147)
D (196)	D (196)	EOT (132)
F (198)	F (198)	ACK (134)
G (199)	G (199)	BEL (135)
H (200)	H (200)	BS (136)
J (202)	J (202)	LF (138)
K (203)	K (203)	VT (139)
L (204)	L (204)	FF (140)
; (187)	+ (171)	; (187)
← (136)	BS (136)	BS (136)
→ (149)	NAK (149)	NAK (149)
Z (218)	Z (218)	SUB (154)
X (216)	X (216)	CAN (152)
C (195)	C (195)	ETX (131)
V (214)	V (214)	SYN (150)
B (194)	B (194)	STX (130)
N (206)	↑ (222)	SO (142)
M (205)	] (221)	CR (141)
, (172)	< (188)	, (172)
. (174)	> (190)	. (174)
/ (175)	? (191)	/ (191)
SPACE (160)	SPACE (160)	SPACE (160)

REPEAT, SHIFT & CTRL ACT ONLY ON OTHER KEYS.
RESET IS DIRECT ACTING. ▒▒▒ = CONTROL COMMAND.
VALUES SHOWN ARE BEFORE STROBE RESET. FOR ASCII EQUIVALENT, SUBTRACT
DECIMAL 128.

Fig. 8-3. Decimal codes for the Apple II keyboard.

Suppose something we do turns out too slow. How can we find out how fast our BASIC is working for us? Fig. 8-2D shows the way to measure the execution time of any BASIC sequence. What you do is repeat the sequence over and over for 10,000 times in a loop. The number of *tens* of seconds it takes to execute the sequence will equal the number of milliseconds the sequence actually took. This is easily timed with a kitchen clock or a stopwatch. Be sure to subtract out the millisecond it takes for the timer loop to cycle with nothing inside the loop.

Hopefully, you will never need this speed measurer. But, if ever you have characters getting ignored or have things taking far too long in your particular program, this how-fast-is-it program can often show you what is holding up the works.

A LOWER-CASE TESTER

Fig. 8-4 shows a simple program that reads the keyboard and puts lower-case characters on the bottom line of the display for us. The program has only one feature—it is short. This makes it handy for initial tests. But since it lacks a cursor and a way to print upper case, and it prints all machine commands on the screen, we'll really need better stuff for anything but checkout.

```
100  FOR CURS = 2000 TO 2039
110     CHAR = PEEK (−16384): IF CHAR < 127 THEN 110
120     POKE (−16368),0
130     IF CHAR > 192 THEN CHAR = CHAR − 160
140     POKE CURS,CHAR
150     NEXT CURS
160  GOTO 100
```

This simple program puts lower-case characters on the bottom display line. Numerals and punctuation appear normally. Use this program only for hardware checkout. CTRL-C restores normal BASIC operation.

Fig. 8-4. A lower-case test program.

The program is a simple loop that progresses across the bottom line addresses 2000 to 2039. We read the keyboard in 110, until a key is pressed. Then we reset the keyboard. If the character has a value greater than decimal 192, we subtract 160 from it to convert it to lower case. For instance, an upper case "A" will have a CHAR value of 193, per Fig. 8-3. Subtract 160 from this to get 33, the lower case "a" needed in Fig. 8-1. We then load the character onto the display in the cursed position. Incrementing the loop with the NEXT CURS instruction in 150 moves us across the screen, while the GOTO 100 in line 160 resets us to the beginning of the line.

A USEFUL DISPLAY PROGRAM

Let's add some stuff to the program in Fig. 8-4 that will make it more useful. We can scroll at the end of the line to move things progressively up on the display. We can decode a RETURN to do the same thing. And, if we can only figure out some way to get both upper- and lower-case characters out of an upper-case keyboard, we are home free toward a simple way to get continuous upper- and lower-case messages displayed.

To trick the keyboard into being something it is not, we'll use the ESCAPE key. We'll set the program up so that under "normal" conditions, you get all lower-case characters. If you hit ESCAPE *once,* only the *next* character will be capitalized. This is just like hitting SHIFT momentarily on a regular typewriter.

If you hit ESCAPE *twice* in a row, the keyboard will *lock* into an upper-case-only mode. This is just like using the LOCK on a regular typewriter. If you are LOCKed into upper case, hitting ESCAPE one more time gets you into lower case once again, just like hitting SHIFT after LOCK on an ordinary typewriter puts you back into lower case. Since we are using software, our ESCAPE commands apply only to the alphabet—everything else stays the same.

This may sound complicated, but it's really simple to use. When and if your Apple II is to have mixed upper and lower case, just use ESCAPE instead of SHIFT to shift the alphabet. Everything else stays the same.

The software behind this is simple enough. We have a variable called SHIFT and a variable called LOCK. Every time a character is entered, it attempts to reset SHIFT to zero and is allowed to do so if LOCK is also a zero. The ESCAPE logic goes like this:

When an ESCAPE key is sensed . . .

1. First you check to see if LOCK was a "1." If LOCK was a "1," this means you want to *release* all caps, so you simply make LOCK a "0" and SHIFT a "0" and go on to the next key.

2. Then you check to see if the *previous* key was *also* an ESCAPE. If it was, SHIFT must be a "1," since no intervening character had a chance to reset SHIFT back to "0." We then make LOCK a "1" and go on to the next key.

3. If you got this far, SHIFT and LOCK must *both* be "0." This means you either want to capitalize only one letter, or else that another ESCAPE will follow to lock. So, make SHIFT a "1" and then go on to the next key.

The new, improved program is shown in Fig. 8-5. This enters full alphabet characters sequentially on the bottom line for us, with full scrolling and carriage return. SHIFT is used for everything already on the keycaps, while ESCAPE is used to pick upper, lower, or mixed cases. Once again, one ESCAPE capitalizes only the next character. Two ESCAPEs capitalize everything until a third ESCAPE resets back to lower case.

The program works the same way the one in Fig. 8-4 does. Line 100 indexes us across the bottom of the screen, while 110 reads the keyboard for us.

Line 120 tests for carriage RETURN and calls for a scroll if one is needed. Line 130 tests for ESCAPE and then does the shift lock

```
 10   REM THIS APPLE INTEGER BASIC PROGRAM DISPLAYS LOWER CASE
      CHARACTERS. USE ESC TWICE FOR SHIFT LOCK. USE ESC ONCE FOR
      SHIFT OR RELEASE.
100   FOR CURS = 2000 TO 2039
110       CHAR = PEEK (−16384): IF CHAR < 127 THEN 110: POKE (−16368),0
120           IF CHAR = 141 THEN 180 : REM CR
130           IF CHAR = 155 THEN 190 : REM ESC
140           IF CHAR > 192 AND SHIFT = 0 THEN CHAR = CHAR − 192
150       POKE CURS, CHAR
160           IF LOCK = 0 THEN SHIFT = 0
170   NEXT CURS
180   CALL −912: GOTO 100: REM SCROLL
190   IF LOCK = 0 THEN 200: LOCK = 0: SHIFT = 0: GOTO 110: REM RELEASE
      LOCK
200   IF SHIFT = 0 THEN 210: LOCK = 1: GOTO 110: REM SET LOCK ESC #2
210   SHIFT = 1: GOTO 110: REM SHIFT ON ESC #1
```

This program may be used to fill the screen with combined upper- and lower-case text via bottom-line entry. SCROLL and RETURN work. There is no visible cursor and no upper screen access.

Fig 8-5. A lower-case display program.

processing in lines 190-210. If shift is not locked, line 140 converts to lower case. Line 150 enters the characters on the screen.

Your Turn:

What does line 160 do in Fig. 8-5? Why is it needed?

Line 170 tells us to pick the next character location to the right. If this happens to be off the screen to the right, we drop out of the loop, do a scroll, and start over.

A FULL-PERFORMANCE LOWER-CASE EDITOR

The previous Gee-Whiz programs are handy to put lower case on an Apple II. But, what we really may want is some full editing system that lets us

* Put any character anywhere on the screen
* Move around anywhere we like
* Insert and delete characters and lines
* Justify ragged or flush right

* Have lines longer than 40 characters
* Be able to transfer into and out of floppy
* Be able to provide hard copy output
* Have an attractive cursor for all characters
* Have no BASIC prompts or unwanted
  scrolls messing up the screen.

Let's look at some of the bits and pieces that will be helpful to build an editor and display system. Then we'll show you a medium-complexity display editor that lets you wander around the screen with a vengeance. From there, you should be able to pick up just about as fancy a text editor as you care to.

Apple Display Memory Locations

The Apple people were among the first to recognize the incredible power and economy of using main memory also as a display memory. They do this by *sharing* each clock cycle so that the computer gets the memory for half a microsecond and the dedicated system timing gets the memory for display uses on the other half.

As you find out pretty fast when you try to stuff things onto the screen, the memory locations are *not* sequential, and they are not all in one piece. How can we find what goes where?

The Apple II has two display pages, one residing at decimal 1024 to 2047 and a second page immediately above. Only the first page is normally used. Fig. 8-6 shows a hex map of the Apple II display memory locations. Their mapping is somewhat similar to the memory repacking done on the KIM systems in *The Cheap Video Cookbook*. Apple chose to stuff three lines per each *half* of a 6502's page of 256 words.

Apple uses a 40-character horizontal line numbered left to right from 0 to 39. They use a 24 row vertical field numbered top to bottom from 0 to 23.

Fig. 8-6 is fine for all us machine-language freaks. But integer BASIC works in decimal numbers, and it's not at all obvious what goes where. So, Fig. 8-7 is a remapping of the Apple II screen showing what portion of the memory goes where on the screen, in decimal numbers. For instance, decimal character location 1706 is the third character from the left on the fourteenth line down from the top.

These sure are strange numbers! They were picked to simplify the internal Apple II system timing. As you can see, if you just try to sequentially put stuff on the screen, you'll put down the top line, then the *ninth* line down, then the *seventeenth*. Then you'll lose eight characters down the drain somewhere. Then onto the second, tenth, and eighteenth lines. Then lose eight more characters. Messy, yes. But a great hardware simplification.

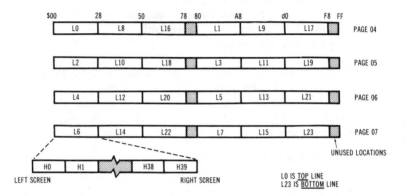

Fig. 8-6. Display memory locations of Apple II shown as hex map.

So, as a general rule, if you can't use hardware to simplify software, then you use software to simplify hardware. One or the other works every time.

	H0	H39
V0	1024	1063
	1152	1191
V2	1280	1319
	1408	1447
V4	1536	1575
	1664	1703
V6	1792	1831
	1920	1959
V8	1064	1103
	1192	1231
V10	1320	1359
	1448	1487
V12	1576	1615
	1704	1743
V14	1832	1871
	1960	1999
V16	1104	1143
	1232	1271
V18	1360	1399
	1488	1527
V20	1616	1655
	1744	1783
V22	1872	1911
	2000	2039

LOCATIONS NOT ON SCREEN

1144 - 1151
1272 - 1279
1400 - 1407
1528 - 1535
1656 - 1663
1784 - 1791
1912 - 1919
2040 - 2047

EACH HORIZONTAL ROW IS NUMBERED SEQUENTIALLY FROM LEFT TO RIGHT.

Fig. 8-7. Display memory locations of Apple II shown as decimal locations.

A programmer would like to have a variable H for the horizontal position with a 0 to 39 range and a variable V for the vertical position ranging from 0 to 23. Obviously, we need a way to get from the H and V locations to the magic display memory addresses.

The Apple II monitor does this in the firmware with a disgustingly elegant sequence starting at hex $FBC1 and called BASCALC. BASCALC takes the H value in $24 and the V value in $25 and puts the result BASL in $28 and BASH in $29. Thus, the programmer uses H and V, while the machine hardware gets to use BASL and BASH, and everybody is happy.

Unfortunately, quite a bit of PEEKing, POKEing, pushing, and shoving is involved to call this sequence from Integer BASIC. Instead, let's find a BASIC way to generate the right addresses.

Fig. 8-8 shows the math needed to find a particular address on the screen. The formulas are in three parts, depending on what third of the screen you happen to be on. To find a screen location, just use one of these formulas, and the results should agree with Fig. 8-7.

You can, of course, program these formulas into Integer BASIC. And it's a fun thing to do. But we need something faster and simpler. Fig. 8-9 shows a table-lookup way to do the same thing. What we do is store the leftmost address for the 24 lines as an array of values called B(V), meaning "Base address for line #V." To this, we add the horizontal value and get a result CURS that has the correct display address for a given H and V.

Note that there are two ways to enter the program. The *first* time you enter, you have to set up the B(V) array and initialize all the values. It's recommended you do this *every* time you clear the screen to make sure this table is intact. After you are sure the table is prop-

---

H = Horizontal Position 0 (Left) to 39 (Right)
V = Vertical Position 0 (Top) to 23 (Bottom)

For Lines 0-7:

Address = 1024 + (128*V) + H

For Lines 8-15:

Address = 1064 + (128*(V − 8)) + H

For Lines 16-23:

Address = 1104 + (128*(V − 16)) + H

Fig. 8-8. One method of calculating Apple II display addresses.

```
     Initial
     enter →    1000      DIM B(64)
                1010      B(0) = 1024: B(1) = 1152: B(2) = 1280: B(3) = 1408:
                          B(4) = 1536: B(5) = 1664: B(6) = 1792: B(7) = 1920
                1020      B(8) = 1064: B(9) = 1192: B(10) = 1320: B(11) = 1448:
                          B(12) = 1576: B(13) = 1704: B(14) = 1832: B(15) = 1960
                1030      B(16) = 1104: B(17) = 1232: B(18) = 1360: B(19) = 1488:
                          B(20) = 1616: B(21) = 1744: B(22) = 1872: B(23) = 2000

     Usual
     enter →    2000      IF V > 23 THEN V = 23: IF V < 0 THEN V = 0
                2010      IF H > 39 THEN H = 39: IF H < 0 THEN H = 0
                2020      CURS = B(V) + H

        For cold start, enter and initialize sequence at 1000.

        To find a location after initialization, enter at 2000.

        CURS will carry the correct display location to the instruction following 2020.
```

Fig. 8-9. An integer BASIC sequence to find Apple II display memory locations.

erly stashed, you can enter at 2000 and do the simple one-line CURS calculation shown at 2020. It is very important to be sure that the V and H values are in fact on the screen. Otherwise, you might end up POKEing a character into memory somewhere off the screen, plowing up a program or some operating system. This is why you should check H and V (lines 2000 and 2010) immediately before you use them.

A Software Cursor

There doesn't seem to be an obvious way to keep Apple II compatibility and be able to use the hardware cursor to wink lower case. So, a software cursor can be used instead. Fig. 8-10 shows how to combine your keyboard scanning with a cursor routine that winks any character on the screen by replacing the character with a solid box, repeating a few times a second.

A single loop is used to both provide a cursor and test for pressed keys. If no key is pressed, the loop continues.

On the first trip through the loop, the cursed character is temporarily saved and is then replaced with a box cursor. On the 12th trip through the loop, the box cursor is removed and replaced with the saved character. On the 24th trip through the loop, the sequence repeats.

So long as no key is pressed, a winking cursor appears on the screen. When a key finally gets hit, the cursor is immediately erased and replaced with the correct character. If things happen to be on the second half of the loop, the character simply replaces itself. At

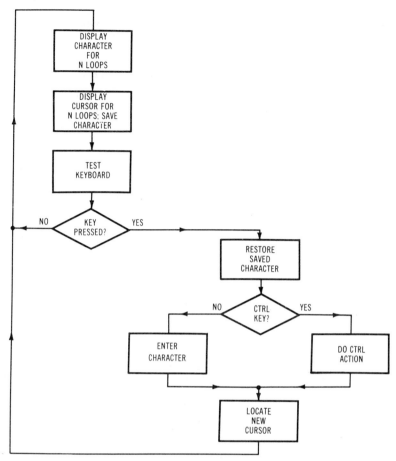

Fig. 8-10. Flowchart for an editing display that combines a winking software cursor within the keyboard testing loop.

any rate, when we are sure we have a pressed key, we make sure the cursor goes away.

The key is then tested to see if it is a character or a machine command. If it's a character, it gets entered. If it's a machine command, the command gets acted on if it is valid and ignored if not.

The new cursor location is found only *after* character entry or machine command actions are complete. The program then jumps back to the main loop, testing for pressed keys and winking the cursor. Cursor winking speed is software adjustable.

One interesting feature of the combined cursor and keycheck loop is that the cursor always goes ON the instant after a new location appears. This is much cleaner looking and easier to follow than the aliasing that sometimes takes place with rapid motions of a hard-ware-blinked, asynchronous cursor.

A FULL DUAL-CASE EDITING SYSTEM

Fig. 8-11 shows a medium-complexity full editing system that puts upper- and lower-case characters anywhere you want on the screen, with full cursor motions. Features included are upper and lower case, clearing, normal entry, cursor right-left-up-down, carriage return, scrolling, erase to end of line, erase to end of paragraph, lower-case shift, and shift lock. Four hooks are provided to interact with your disc or hard-copy system, or to add other features. It's a simple matter to add all the bells and whistles you want.

In 100 through 200, we set up the base address file for our screen address finder. These values are rechecked every time the screen is erased. Step 140 gives us a clear screen on startup and when called

```
 10   REM EDITING DUAL CASE DISPLAY SYSTEM FOR APPLE II
 20   REM CLEAR = CTRL X           CURSOR RIGHT = RIGHT ARROW
          SHIFT = ESCAPE           CURSOR LEFT = LEFT ARROW
          LOCK = ESCAPE X2         CURSOR UP = CTRL A
 30   REM UNLOCK = ESCAPE          CURSOR DOWN = CTRL B
          RETURN = RETURN          ERASE EOL = CTRL D
          HOOKS = CTRL Q,R,S,T     ERASE EOP = CTRL W

100   DIM B(64): REM  SET UP BASE ADDRESS TABLE
110   B(0) = 1024: B(1) = 1152: B(2) = 1280: B(3) = 1408:
      B(4) = 1536: B(5) = 1664: B(6) = 1792: B(7) = 1920
      B(8) = 1064: B(9) = 1192: B(10) = 1320: B(11) = 1448
120   B(12) = 1576: B(13) = 1704: B(14) = 1832: B(15) = 1960
      B(16) = 1104: B(17) = 1232: B(18) = 1360: B(19) = 1488
      B(20) = 1616: B(21) = 1744: B(22) = 1872: B(23) = 2000

140   CALL −936: H = 0: V = 0: REM CLEAR SCREEN; HOME CURSOR

160   IF V > 23 THEN V = 23: IF V < 0 THEN V = 0
170   IF H > 39 THEN H = 39: IF H < 0 THEN H = 0
180   CURS = B(V) + H: REM FIND CURS ADDRESS AFTER VALID V,H

200   CCNT = 0
210   CCNT = CCNT + 1
220   IF CCNT > 1 THEN 240: CSTR = PEEK (CURS)
230       POKE (CURS), 63: REM SAVE CHAR; WRITE CURSOR
240   IF CCNT = 12 THEN POKE CURS,CSTR
250   IF CCNT > 23 THEN CCNT = 0: REM UNWINK CURSOR

260   CHAR = PEEK (−16384): IF CHAR < 127 THEN 210
270       POKE (−16368),0: POKE CURS,CSTR
280       IF CHAR < 160 THEN 1000: REM CTRL KEY TEST
```

Fig. 8-11. A full lower-case Apple II

for. It uses the clearing sequence already in the monitor. Steps 160 through 180 find valid cursor locations for us, starting with H and V positions.

Our combination cursor loop and keyboard test appears in 200 through 280. A cursor counting variable, CCNT, counts from 0 to 24 for us. On count 1, the character being cursed is stored temporarily as CSTR. The cursor box (an ASCII 63, DEL) is loaded in its place. On CCNT count 12, the original character is replaced. On CCNT count 24, the cycle repeats. Meanwhile, the keyboard has been checked for a pressed key 24 times. You can think of CCNT as a divide-by-24 counter that is clocked by the keyboard testing. By changing the numbers, you can change the winking rate and the ratio of cursor to character time.

Once a key is pressed, we reset the keyboard strobe and make sure the cursed character has been put back where it belongs. Step 270 does this for us. Then, in 280, we test for CTRL keys.

```
300   IF (CHAR > 192 AND SHIFT = 0) THEN CHAR = CHAR − 160: REM
      LOWER CASE ONLY IF UNSHIFTED CAPITAL LETTER
310   IF LOCK = 0 THEN SHIFT = 0: REM RETURN TO LOWER CASE IF UNLOCKED

400   POKE CURS, CHAR: REM ENTER CHAR
410       H = H + 1: IF H < 40 THEN 160: H = 0: REM ADJ H POS
420       V = V + 1: IF V > 23 THEN CALL −912: GOTO 160: REM
          ADJ V POS; SCROLL IF OFF SCREEN

1000  POKE 36,H: POKE 37,V: REM TRANSFER HV TO MONITOR FOR EOS
1010  IF CHAR = 152 THEN 100: REM CLEAR AND HOME ON CTRL X
1020  IF CHAR # 141 THEN 1030: H = 0: V = V + 1: IF V > 23 THEN CALL −912:
      REM CARRIAGE RETURN. SCROLL IF OFF SCREEN.
1030  IF CHAR = 136 THEN H = H − 1: REM BACKSPACE ON ARROW
1040  IF CHAR = 139 THEN H = H + 1: REM ADVANCE ON ARROW
1050  IF CHAR = 129 THEN V = V − 1: REM CURSOR UP ON CTRL A
1060  IF CHAR = 130 THEN V = V + 1: REM CURSOR DOWN ON CTRL B
1070  IF CHAR = 155 THEN 2000: REM ESCAPE SHIFT SEQUENCE
1080  IF CHAR #132 THEN 1090: FOR H1 = H TO 39: POKE (B(V) + H),63:
      NEXT H1: REM ERASE TO END OF LINE ON CTRL D
1090  IF CHAR = 151 THEN CALL −958: REM MONITOR ERASE EOS ON CTRL W
1100  IF CHAR = 145 THEN 160: REM SPARE HOOK ON CTRL Q DC1
1110  IF CHAR = 146 THEN 160: REM SPARE HOOK ON CTRL R DC2
1120  IF CHAR = 147 THEN 160: REM SPARE HOOK ON CTRL S DC3
1130  IF CHAR = 148 THEN 160: REM SPARE HOOK ON CTRL T DC4
1140  GOTO 160: REM RESUME KEYBOARD SCAN ON UNUSED CTRL COMMAND

2000  IF LOCK = 0 THEN 2010: LOCK = 0: SHIFT = 0: GOTO 160: REM RELEASE LOCK
2010  IF SHIFT = 0 THEN 2020: LOCK = 1: GOTO 160: REM SET LOCK ON
      SECOND ESCAPE
2020  SHIFT = 1: GOTO 160: REM SHIFT ON FIRST ESCAPE
```

editing display system.

If the pressed key happens to be a character, step 300 decides whether lower or upper case is to be displayed. Step 310 releases shift after a capital letter unless the shift is locked.

Actual character entry takes place in 400, while the cursor is adjusted in 410 and 420. If we go off-screen to the right, H is reset to 0 and V is incremented down-screen by one. If V goes off-screen, we call for a scroll, using the firmware scroll sequence in the monitor. After repositioning the cursor, the program returns to the main cursor and keycheck loop by jumping to 160. At this time, the cursor starts winking in the new location.

CTRL keys are processed in steps 1000 to 1040. Most are obvious. Step 1000 is needed so you can use the firmware erase-to-end-of-screen in the monitor; this step transfers the BASIC H and V values to the slots in the monitor where they are needed. Unfortunately, the monitor's erase-to-end-of-line firmware sequence doesn't seem to be as useful (it doesn't calculate its own base address), so this shorter erase sequence is done on our own in step 1080.

The spare hooks are shown in 1100 through 1130. Simply replace 160 (return-to-keyboard-loop) with the location you need for access to your disc, printer, or other program. Around a dozen other hooks can be added, just by picking new CTRL commands from Fig. 8-3. Remember that CTRL-C is excluded, as this gets you back to the Integer BASIC operating system.

Should no valid CTRL key be found, the jump in 1140 puts us back into the keyboard checking business.

Steps 2000 through 2020 do the now familiar ESCAPE processing for the lower-case shift lock. As before, a single ESCAPE gives one capital letter. Two in a row locks us into capitals only. Should we be locked into capitals only, the next ESCAPE unlocks back to lower case.

Some Bells and Whistles

You can add just about anything you like to this editor program. For easy editing, you might like to add an additional keypad that generates all the motion commands with a single keystroke each. This heavyweight modification would be handy for word processing, typesetting, and so on.

It's fairly obvious how you would add things like diagonal and cursor home motions, cursor OFF-ON, tabs, etc. To get into really fancy editing, you have to be able to add and delete characters. How you do this depends on the rules you choose to set up for your particular system. Several full editors are available as software packages that may be of help to you.

A simple example of a delete-character subroutine is shown in Fig. 8-12. Starting at the cursor plus one, every character on the line

```
4000   FOR H1 = H to 38
4010      CURM = B(V) + H1
4020      POKE CURM,PEEK (CURM +1): REM MOVE ONE LEFT
4030   NEXT H1
4040   POKE (B(V)+39),160; REM BLANK END CHAR
4050   RETURN
```

The subroutine starts at the cursed location and moves everything on its
own line left one character. The last character is erased.

**Fig. 8-12. A BASIC subroutine to delete a single character on the
Apple II display.**

is moved one to the left. When this is finished, the last character will
be repeated *twice*. The duplicate end character is then erased. The
repeated moves take place in the 4000 to 4030 loop, while the end
character erasure happens in step 4040. This particular delete-character sequence operates only on a single line. Lines farther down the
screen are not affected.

Inserting extra characters is a harder problem, since everything
has to be shoved around the screen to make enough room. Once
again, you have to pick the shoving rules you want to use for your
particular editing needs.

One possible insert-a-character subroutine is shown in Fig. 8-13.
This uses a rule that says it will keep bumping characters until it
finds a line whose last character is a space. Usually, this will be the
line you are working on, but if not, characters will keep getting
bumped until a space at the end of a line is found. Then the bumping stops and the rest of the screen stays the way it was.

Here are the steps involved in this insert-a-character sequence:

1. A check is made to find out how many lines are involved until
   one is found with a space at the end (steps 3000 to 3040).
2. Everything on the bottom-most line to be bumped is shoved
   one to the right. Remember that at least the rightmost character is a space on this line.
3. There will be a double character at the left of the line, provided it's not the one that had the cursor on it. This double
   character is replaced with the last character on the previous
   line (3160, 3170).
4. The process repeats as often as needed for all but the top line
   to be bumped. The loop is done with step 3100.
5. The line with the cursor on it gets characters bumped only from
   the cursor to the end of the line and has no need to borrow a
   character from a previous line. The change in policy for the
   cursed line is handled by step 3110.
6. Finally, everything will be bumped, but a duplicate character

will remain at the cursed location. This dupe is erased in step 3190.

This is a fairly simple inserter that works fairly well and reasonably fast. If you don't like its rules, change them to suit yourself. The sequence is rather slow if you use it over and over again as you might while justifying a whole page of text. You should be able to speed it up bunches if you get into this sort of thing. The rule selected does have one possible bug in it—repeated insertions can swallow end spaces and run words together, as the next line bumping takes place with a character in the last slot and does not if a space is there. Requiring *two* spaces at line end may help. There are all sorts of other options, depending on what you want your particular editor to do.

Your Turn:

Add the following bells and whistles to your editing program:

* **Ragged justify right**—in which whole words are never broken on the right side of the screen and you can continuously type without carriage returns.

* **Flush justify right**—in which everything ends up square on the right side of the screen as needed for typesetting. What hyphenation and short-line rules will you use for this?

* **Variable character lines**—in which you can go as long as 80 characters for text and form-letter editing.

As a hint to longer lines, just select *pairs* of lines when they are needed, and act on these line pairs. Thus you should be able to output up to 80 characters for a business letter or a manuscript to your hard copy, while still viewing the results on a normal 40-character Apple screen. We'll leave the details up to you since the results are application specific. Have fun.

```
3000   V2 = 0: H2 = 0
3010   FOR V1 = V TO 23: REM FIND FIRST END SPACE
3020      CEND = PEEK (B(V1 + 39))
3030      IF CEND = 160 THEN 3100
3040      V2 = V2 + 1: NEXT V1
3100   FOR V1 = (V2 +V) TO V STEP −1: REM: NEXT LINE
3110      IF V1 = V THEN H2 = H
3120      FOR H1 = 38 TO H2 STEP −1: REM SHIFT A LINE
3130         CURM = B(V1) + H1
3140         POKE (CURM + 1), PEEK (CURM)
3150         NEXT H1
3160      IF V1 = V THEN 3180: REM MOVE (V1 − 1), 39 TO V1,0
3170         POKE B(V1),PEEK (B(V1 − 1) + 39)
3180      NEXT V1
3190   POKE (B(V) + H), 160: REM: DELETE CHARACTER
3200   RETURN
```

The subroutine starts at the cursed location. It finds the first available line with a space at the end, and then moves all intervening characters as needed. The cursed character is then erased.

Fig. 8-13. A BASIC subroutine to insert a single character on the Apple II display.

FURTHER HARDWARE MODS

Some of the more popular Apple II software uses the screen reversal feature. This software may not be reasonably displayed with the hardware mods we've shown you so far. The checkbook program is one example, where deposits are shown reversed as black-on-white numerals. Is there some way we can still run these programs *and* have lower case?

One obvious way is to use a switch to select *either* screen reversal *or* lower case. Fig. 8-14 shows where this switch goes. Only an spst switch and a resistor need be added to the existing modifications. This switch can be mounted along the right side of the circuit board far enough to the rear that it is easily reached. A miniature slide switch held in place with double-stick foam should do the trick.

The switchover works by providing a DL6 signal to A11 and A13 for upper case, and a logic "1" for screen reversal. If we provide DL6, we get lower case since A11 forces the lower case ASCII bit 6 output, and A13 inhibits screen reversal. If we provide a logic "1," lower case is inhibited, and reversal is allowed when it is called for.

You put the switch in the REVERSE position for programs that need reverse video continuously displayed. You put the switch in the LOWER CASE position when you must display lower case.

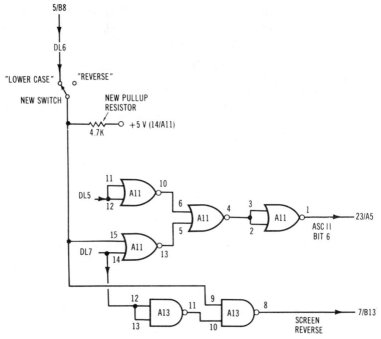

Fig. 8-14. A changeover switch and pullup resistor may be added to give choice of lower case or reverse video displays.

Your Turn:

The character generator in Module "A" also will display CTRL characters if you make DL5 and ASCII bit 6 both *zeros.* When would you want to display control characters? How can you do this? Can you eliminate the changeover switch and re-place it with a series of software flags that gives you everything at once—reversal—full case blinking—lower case—CTRL displayed on command—and—invisibility on existing software?

Note that you can also use other character generators by suitably changing the pins around. There's also a lower-case 2513 you can piggyback onto the existing upper-case one.

You can also use your own character generator by burning your own 2716 EPROM like we did for the music display a few chapters back. This will take a different adaptor.

The advantages of the EPROM are that you can get any character and lots of graphics symbols that you like on a hardware basis. For instance, instead of the awkward treatment of the descenders on the lower-case "g," "p," and so on, you could use 5×7 upper case for caps and 5×5 upper case for lower case. This can be both legible and attractive.

There is one limitation to the 2716 when you use it with an only slightly modified Apple II. With the Apple II, only five output lines are used, with the remaining three being permanent blanks. Unless you rework the output video, your 2716 would be more suited to new characters than to graphics symbols that have to butt against each other.

APPENDIX **A**

More Character
Generator Details

EPROM MEMORY (2K × 8)

2716
(Intel)

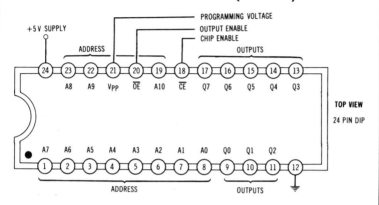

This single-supply, nonvolatile memory of 2048 words of eight bits each may be electrically programmed or reprogrammed, and may be erased with strong ultraviolet light.

To *read*, apply +5 volts ground to supply pins and +5 volts to the programming input VPP. Bring output enable OE and chip enable CE low. Binary addressing of address lines A0 through A10 selects one of the words. The selected word appears as data on outputs Q0 through Q7.

To *erase*, apply short-wavelength ultraviolet light through the top quartz window, using a special lamp. *Eye damage can result from uv light.*

To *begin programming*, bring OE high and CE low. Raise VPP to +25 volts from a source current limited to 40 milliamperes. Always apply VPP *after* supply power. Always remove VPP *before* supply power.

To *continue programming*, apply the desired address to A0 through A10. Apply the word to be programmed to Q0 through Q7 *using these outputs as programming data inputs.* Then, with data and address stable, bring CE high and then low again. The CE high time must be exactly 50 milliseconds.

Chip Enable CE should be held low except for the 50-millisecond high programming time, once per address. Do NOT hold CE high. DO return VPP low at the end of programming.

In the *read mode only*, CE may be brought high to float outputs for tri-state access.

Access time is 400 nanoseconds. Supply current (read) is 60 milliamperes.

Note that the *Texas Instruments* 2716 is not a standard 2716. The *TI* TMS 2516 is equivalent to the industry standard 2716.

(USED IN TVT MODULE "E")

CHARACTER GENERATOR
(5 × 7, Row Scan, Upper & Lower Case)

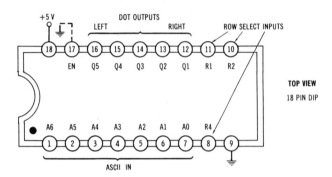

This circuit provides the dot patterns needed for raster scan display of characters. It gives a 5 × 7 dot matrix of the full 128 character ASCII set. It is intended for normal tv row scanning.

In usual operation, +5 volts and ground are applied to the supply pins, and the EN input is *grounded*. ASCII code is input to pins 1 through 7. Row timing is applied to pins 8, 10, and 11. A 000 row timing input outputs an all blank top row. 001 outputs the top dot row, 010 the second, down to 111 that outputs the bottom, or seventh dot row.

Outputs are usually routed to a video shift register for serial conversion. The outputs are arranged so that the leftmost dot Q5 is nearest the *output* of the serial shift register.

The character set includes 32 upper case, 32 numerics, 32 lower case, and 32 machine command symbols. The lower case g, j, p, q, and y appear higher than the others so they will fit in the matrix. Machine command symbols usually are an arrow, a pair of small upper-case characters, or something similar.

If the EN input is made high, the outputs are floated. A cursor may be provided by using the stored cursor symbol DEL or by pulling the outputs high and raising EN. A blank output is provided by using the ASCII blank symbol or by forcing the R1, R2, and R4 line timing inputs to all zeros.

Access time is 500 nanoseconds after all inputs are stable. *Note that at least 500 nanoseconds of delay must be provided before output information is accepted following any input change.*

Supply current is 130 milliamperes.

(USED IN TVT MODULE "A")

Pinouts of Selected ICs

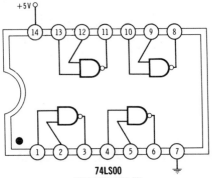

74LS00
QUAD NAND GATE, TTL
(14-PIN DIP, TOP VIEW)

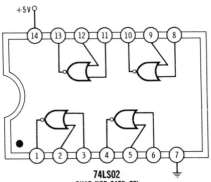

74LS02
QUAD NOR GATE, TTL
(14-PIN DIP, TOP VIEW)

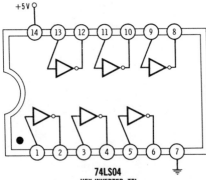

74LS04
HEX INVERTER, TTL
(14-PIN DIP, TOP VIEW)

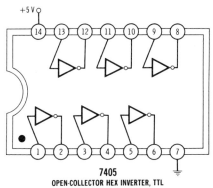

7405
OPEN-COLLECTOR HEX INVERTER, TTL
(14-PIN DIP, TOP VIEW)

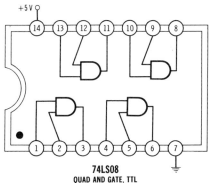

74LS08
QUAD AND GATE, TTL
(14-PIN DIP, TOP VIEW)

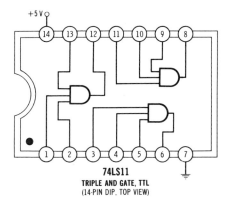

74LS11
TRIPLE AND GATE, TTL
(14-PIN DIP, TOP VIEW)

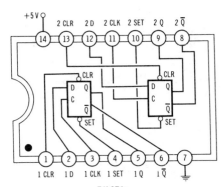

74LS74
DUAL D FLIP-FLOP, TTL
(14-PIN DIP, TOP VIEW)

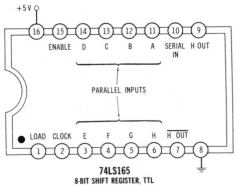

74LS165
8-BIT SHIFT REGISTER, TTL
(16-PIN DIP, TOP VIEW)

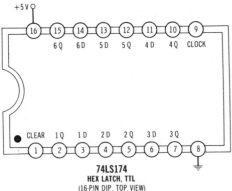

74LS174
HEX LATCH, TTL
(16-PIN DIP, TOP VIEW)

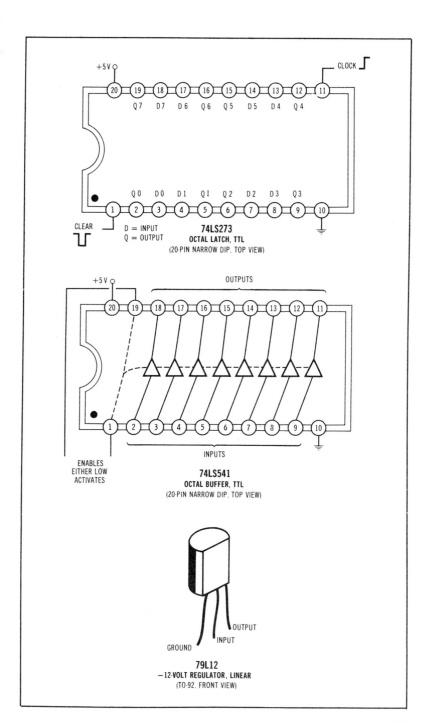

+5V

CLOCK

20 19 18 17 16 15 14 13 12 11

Q 7 D 7 D 6 Q 6 Q 5 D 5 D 4 Q 4

Q 0 D 0 D 1 Q 1 Q 2 D 2 D 3 Q 3

1 2 3 4 5 6 7 8 9 10

CLEAR

D = INPUT
Q = OUTPUT

74LS273
OCTAL LATCH, TTL
(20-PIN NARROW DIP, TOP VIEW)

+5V

OUTPUTS

20 19 18 17 16 15 14 13 12 11

1 2 3 4 5 6 7 8 9 10

INPUTS

ENABLES
EITHER LOW
ACTIVATES

74LS541
OCTAL BUFFER, TTL
(20-PIN NARROW DIP, TOP VIEW)

OUTPUT
INPUT
GROUND

79L12
−12-VOLT REGULATOR, LINEAR
(TO-92, FRONT VIEW)

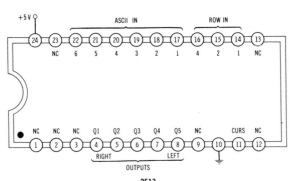

2513
CHARACTER GENERATOR, NMOS
(24-PIN DIP, TOP VIEW)

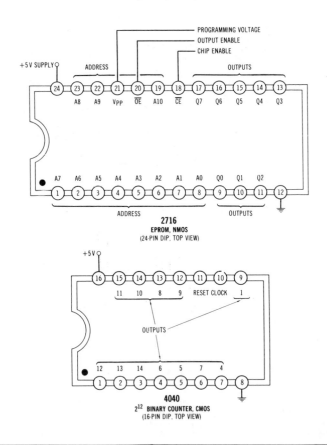

2716
EPROM, NMOS
(24-PIN DIP, TOP VIEW)

4040
2^{12} **BINARY COUNTER, CMOS**
(16-PIN DIP, TOP VIEW)

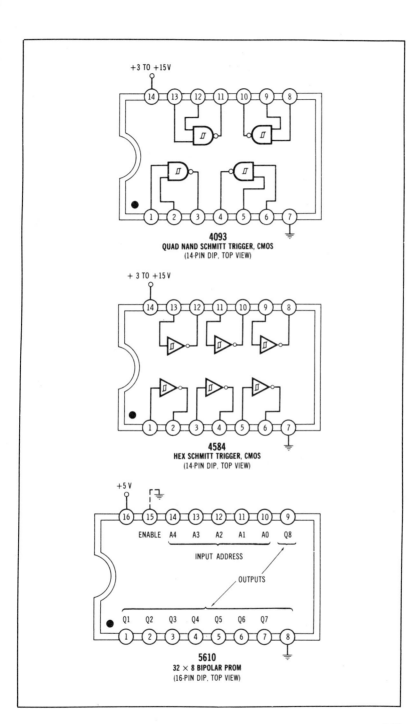

+3 TO +15 V

4093
QUAD NAND SCHMITT TRIGGER, CMOS
(14-PIN DIP, TOP VIEW)

+ 3 TO +15 V

4584
HEX SCHMITT TRIGGER, CMOS
(14-PIN DIP, TOP VIEW)

+5 V

ENABLE   A4   A3   A2   A1   A0   Q8

INPUT ADDRESS

OUTPUTS

Q1   Q2   Q3   Q4   Q5   Q6   Q7

5610
32 × 8 BIPOLAR PROM
(16-PIN DIP, TOP VIEW)

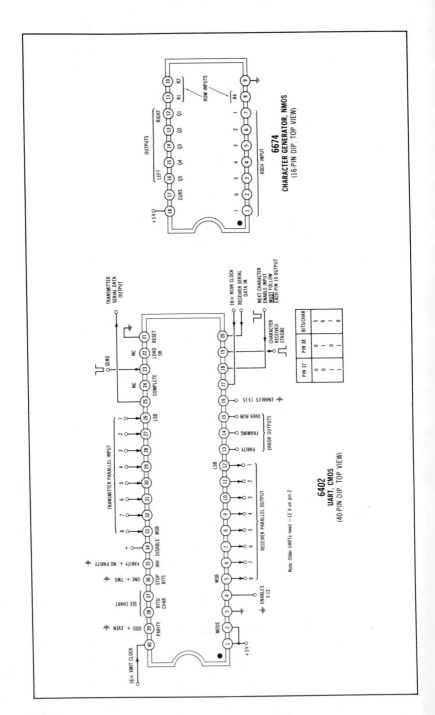

6674
CHARACTER GENERATOR, NMOS
(16-PIN DIP, TOP VIEW)

6402
UART, CMOS
(40-PIN DIP, TOP VIEW)

Note: Older UARTs need −12 V on pin 2.

PIN 37	PIN 38	BITS/CHAR
0	0	5
0	1	6
1	0	7
1	1	8

APPENDIX **C**

Printed Circuit Patterns

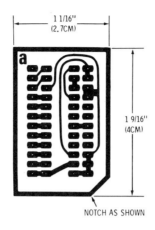

Fig. C-1. Module A (Alphanumeric) foil pattern.

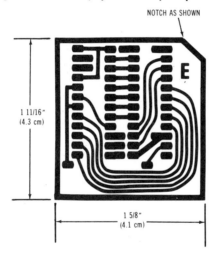

Fig. C-2. Module E (EPROM) foil pattern.